How to Create, Sell, and Teach Online Courses

Winning Techniques to Help You Create, Sell, and Impart Your Knowledge and Expertise Online

Dr. Sadiyo Siad

Dedication

This book is dedicated to our amazing team of teachers, who have been working with us both online and offline at <u>Hano Academy</u>, <u>www.eLearningX.org</u>, our other distance-learning platforms, and <u>Hano Technical University</u>.

You guys kept me learning and finding solutions to improve our services and contributions to tech education.

Thank you!

Acknowledgment

I am profoundly grateful for the completion of this book, *"How to Create, Sell, and Teach Online Courses: Winning Techniques to Help You Create, Sell, and Impart Your Knowledge and Expertise Online."* The journey of creating this comprehensive guide would not have been possible without the support, encouragement, and dedication of many individuals.

First and foremost, I extend my heartfelt gratitude to my family and friends for their unwavering belief in my abilities and constant encouragement throughout this endeavor. Your enthusiasm and motivation have been the driving force behind the completion of this book.

I would like to express my sincere appreciation to my mentors, colleagues, and fellow educators who shared their insights, experiences, and expertise in the realm of online education. Your guidance has been invaluable in shaping the content and strategies that are presented in this book.

I am indebted to the numerous online course creators and entrepreneurs who have paved the way in the online education landscape. Your successes, challenges, and innovative approaches have inspired the techniques and methodologies shared within these pages.

A special thanks goes to my editors and the entire publishing team for their dedication and meticulous work in refining and polishing the content to ensure its clarity and coherence.

Last but not least, I want to acknowledge each reader who picks up this book. Your curiosity and commitment to personal and professional growth are what make educational endeavors like this meaningful.

This book is a product of collaboration, dedication, and a shared passion for harnessing the power of educational technology, specifically online education. I hope that it serves as a valuable resource to guide you on your journey of creating, selling, and teaching online courses.

I also offer online training, coaching, and mentoring services. If you require any of my other services, please don't hesitate to contact my team to schedule an appointment.

With heartfelt appreciation,

Dr. Sadiyo Siad

About the Author

Born in the horn of Africa, where the need for almost everything is immense, and pursued her education in Denmark and the UK, Dr. Sadiyo Siad stands as an exceptional entrepreneur, far from the ordinary, and not your typical success story; she is undoubtedly a woman on a mission.

Her journey began as an out-of-school child. The tumultuous backdrop of the Somali civil war forced her to become an internally displaced person (IDP) and, later, a refugee, first in Kenya and then in Denmark. Amidst these trials, she navigated an arranged marriage as a teenage girl, an unfortunate situation that eventually escalated into domestic violence. Undeterred, she triumphed over each adversity.

Despite these hurdles, she achieved a remarkable feat, obtaining five university degrees, including a Ph.D. and two master's degrees, all while confronting dyslexia. Today, she is the director of multiple six-figure social enterprises with aplomb.

Dr. Sadiyo Siad is a fervent BELIEVER, her unwavering strength and resilience propelling her to endure and thrive amidst life's adversities. Her commitment to harmonizing her actions with her passion and purpose empowers her to embrace life fully.

Her journey is proof that extraordinary success can be achieved through relentless determination, ceaseless hard work, unwavering resilience, steadfast hope, prayer, unwavering belief, and boundless patience.

As a serial social entrepreneur, adeptly leveraging technology for sustainable businesses, Dr. Sadiyo's endeavors have significantly contributed to diverse realms: economics, peace-building, healthcare, and education, encompassing technical and STEM (Science, Technology, Engineering, and Mathematics) education, TVET skills training, employment, social development, and human capital advancement mechanisms in Somalia.

Guided by the 3 E's model (Empowerment, Education, and Employment) coupled with the 3 H's framework (Head, Heart, and Hands), her overarching aim is to support and enhance livelihoods sustainably and holistically. She has pioneered innovative initiatives in Europe and Africa, bolstering sustainable economic growth and fervently seeking opportunities to bring visionary ideas to life.

Disclaimer

As you may have read about my bio, I am wholeheartedly on a mission driven by my passion, commitment, and a deep desire to create a lasting legacy. This endeavor is not just for myself but also for those who have joined our journey to make an inclusive, lasting impact on disadvantaged individuals.

I aspire to see this book achieve the prestigious status of a New York Times bestseller, and I firmly believe that, with your invaluable support, this ambitious goal can be realized by recommending the purchase of this book to your colleagues, friends, family, and your local library.

The proceeds generated from the sales of this book will serve a purpose beyond its pages. Specifically, the sales will be directed toward establishing Hano Technical University, a venture close to my heart. Currently, the university operates from rented premises, which limits its capacity to flourish and provide the best possible education to our students. By contributing to this book's success, you are supporting the dissemination of knowledge and actively participating in the realization of a tangible and transformative educational initiative.

I want to express my deepest gratitude for your involvement in this journey. Together, we can make a meaningful impact on the world of education and contribute to the betterment of countless lives.

Thank you for joining me in this endeavor.

Preface

The importance of delivering high-value online courses should not be understated, especially as it allows students to learn from a greater variety of educators who otherwise would not be available to them. This is particularly the case in developing countries where there is a great need for quality education and training to meet the needs of the modern world. As a result, I wanted to provide a framework that could be used to create, sell, and teach quality online courses.

The idea of undertaking online education first came to my mind in 2011 when I visited Somalia. It was a monumental trip for me as I was returning for the first time after having spent almost 19 years away from my birth country. What immediately caught my attention was the low quality of education that was being imparted to the students.

This wasn't an issue in just one or two establishments; it was prevalent throughout the country. In trying to address this problem, I faced a major challenge – improving accessibility for all. This prompted my idea to establish <u>Hano Academy</u> to provide high-quality education for adults and later <u>Hano Technical University</u>.

However, a major stumbling block was the lack of professional and qualified educators because most had left the country because of the civil war. Additionally, it was difficult to hire professionals from abroad, considering the situation in Somalia, particularly in the aftermath of the civil war, as the country was a highly volatile and unsafe place to live.

I considered utilizing online teaching software to help minimize this disparity in accessibility to education. In my search for the right software, I faced disappointment. None that I came across could deliver what I had in mind.

The only educational online platform that I knew of was Blackboard. However, at the time, Blackboard was not designed to provide an engaging and supportive online application that could fully support students. Blackboard was specifically made to host lecture notes and a way to submit coursework and take multiple-choice structured exams.

Consequently, I began considering alternatives, searching for software and platforms similar to Blackboard. This eventually led me to establish Hano Academy in 2014, which entailed hiring professionals who were not available within the country.

Unfortunately, another problem emerged as many of the professionals we had acquired were unfamiliar with running online courses. This resulted in me learning how to train professionals in creating and delivering online courses; thus, Hano Group, which includes Hano Academy, Hano Connect, and Hano Technical University, has benefitted over 40,000 learners and over 600 staff since its establishment.

The totality of these experiences and events has prompted me to write this book on creating, teaching, and selling online courses and package a Master Class Online Training Webinar so that an even greater number of people may benefit from my knowledge and expertise.

With this potential on the horizon, I foresee that you, as the reader of this book, will not only acquire knowledge but also unleash a tenfold impact on your income and returns by harnessing the online sale of your expertise.

I hope this book proves to be a very informative and helpful resource.

Contents

Chapter 1: Why is Online Teaching Important?

How we communicate with each other, facilitate access, and share information has been significantly changed by the internet due to how fast the world has evolved. The use of technology in teaching is no longer an issue - the problem now lies in how teachers need to acknowledge and understand how the world is already developing and understand the significance of online literacy and the role that collaboration and online engagement play in student learning and their future workplace environment.

Technology can be difficult to keep pace with because it constantly changes. However, teachers/facilitators must understand and keep pace with it. Therefore, focusing on this aspect goes hand-in-hand with developing effective pedagogical strategies for online teaching rather than concentrating on the technology itself.

The concept of traditional education has changed radically within the last couple of years. Being physically present in a classroom is no longer the only learning option, at least not with the rise of the internet and new technologies. Nowadays, people have access to a quality education whenever and wherever they want, as long as they can get online.

We are now entering a new era: the revolution of online education.

To get a clearer understanding of this, we must take a closer look at the benefits that online teaching can offer.

Advantages of Online Teaching

As technology advances and user experience improves, so does online education's popularity. It's been proven to be a successful learning method and offers many different benefits compared to traditional education. While it is beneficial, it also has certain challenges. Understanding the advantages of online learning is essential because it could help people make big decisions regarding themselves or their children.

The following are some of the most notable advantages of online teaching.

Flexibility

Teaching online has benefits like increased time flexibility. This means teaching can occur at any time, which is more convenient and productive for teachers and students.

Students often find it easier to work at their own pace within a given time and framework. Lessons taught through online teaching and learning can easily be broken into smaller portions of time and provide the students ample time to reflect on what they have learned.

It means there's room for a schedule that fits everyone's agenda.

As a result, using an online educational platform allows for a better balance of work and studies, so there's no need to give anything up. Studying online teaches vital time-management skills, which makes finding an excellent work-study balance easier. Having a shared agenda between the student and teacher can also prompt both parties to accept new responsibilities and have more autonomy.

Online learning considers an individual's learning pattern. Every student learns differently, and in traditional education, students must adapt to the pace of the class or be left behind, but that is not the case with online learning.

Traditional learning methods allow teachers to decide how they will convey information to their students, but online learning gives students control over their education. We all learn differently; some prefer quiet study, others like interactive tasks and being challenged under pressure.

With online learning, students have time to learn concepts differently. Once they feel prepared, they can then take online tests or ask their parents or people around them to challenge them on what they have learned.

Enhanced Accessibility

Online learning allows increased accessibility; hence, learning can occur anywhere. Online education enables the teacher to teach students anywhere. This can be at home, at work, while traveling, at coffee shops, or anywhere at all, and can include students and teachers from diverse geographical locations.

Online education enables one to study or teach from anywhere in the world. So, there's no need to commute from one place to another or follow a rigid schedule. Learners have more freedom to work at their own pace, which improves their learning experience and helps them build a better understanding of their teacher.

This is also important for the teacher because it helps them structure their classes to suit the individual learning requirements of each learner. The outcome of such online learning/teaching improves grades and offers a more enjoyable experience for the student and the teacher.

Students learn better and feel more comfortable learning in an environment of their choosing. This isn't always possible in a classroom, but it is one of the key advantages of online learning. Students understand where they work best, whether in the library, at home, or elsewhere.

Being able to take a laptop or tablet into their ideal working environment helps students maximize their potential and gain the most from their education. Everyone works differently, and some students may prefer the classroom, but for those who don't, this flexibility can positively impact how they absorb information and help them improve their grades.

Saves Money

On top of that, not only does one save time, but they also save money, which can be spent on other priorities. The virtual classroom is also available anywhere there's an internet connection; an excellent way to take advantage of this is to travel.

For example, if one is studying abroad and wants a job, online education is a great choice; there's no reason to give up working or studying while exploring new and exotic places.

Online learning/teaching tends to be affordable and more cost-effective than traditional education. With online learning, one doesn't have to move from one place to another, thereby using transport. Moreover, online learning gives one a wide range of payment options, in instalments or per class. This allows for better budget management.

Many students may also be subject to discounts or scholarships, so the price is rarely high. Also, there are plenty of scholarships available for online studies these days. In other words, the monetary investment is less, but the results can be better than other options. One can also save money on the commute and class materials, which are often available at no cost online.

Relevant to Current Society

Online education has come in handy in giving learning a new relevance in our current society, and even if people are busy with their daily lives, they can still choose to study during their leisure time. It also provides opportunities to share and access information more easily and readily.

This means that teachers and students from different parts of the world can join online communities of practice in their own areas of study/profession, which allows them to venture more into their areas of interest.

Helps Gain New Perspectives

One of the other advantages of online learning is it can connect students and teachers worldwide. With traditional education, location dictates which classes one could sign up for. This isn't the case with online learning. One can sign up for classes all over the world, providing a more in-depth understanding of the global industry and helping children build their network and develop an international mindset.

Gaining different perspectives and learning about different cultures also aids children's critical thinking skills. This highlights the importance of online learning for students because it can open the door to new opportunities and help them develop skills that will serve them well in their future careers.

Access to Better Resources

With online learning, one can access a vast array of resources and information from online sources and from others who have experience in the industry of their interest. There's often access to diverse material such as videos, photos, and e-books online as well, and tutors can also integrate other formats like forums or discussions to improve their lessons.

And this extra content is available anytime, anywhere, offering a more dynamic and tailor-made education. This can enhance students' learning experiences and provide opportunities for cross-disciplinary, cross-cultural, and cross-campus collaboration. These learning experiences can be local, national, regional, or global and can be enriched by increased interaction and engagement, peer feedback, and group work skills.

Expanding Access for Remote and Underserved Communities

Online teaching has emerged as a lifeline for students residing in remote or underserved communities, offering a ray of hope in regions where educational opportunities were once scarce. It serves as a bridge, effectively closing the geographical gaps that have long hindered access to quality education. This transformation in the educational landscape is particularly invaluable for areas grappling with a shortage of qualified teachers and limited educational infrastructure.

In remote and rural regions, traditional education often falls short due to the inherent challenges of limited access to schools, colleges, and qualified instructors. These geographical barriers have historically posed significant obstacles to the pursuit of knowledge. However, online education transcends these physical boundaries, providing a promising and inclusive solution to enhance learning opportunities in underserved communities.

This digital evolution allows students in remote and rural areas to access educational resources, courses, and expert instruction that would have otherwise remained beyond their reach. It liberates them from the constraints of geographic isolation, offering the promise of a brighter educational future.

As a result, online teaching contributes not only to individual empowerment but also to these communities' economic and social development. By providing access to quality education, online teaching fosters a more knowledgeable and skilled workforce, which, in turn, can positively impact local industries and services. It opens doors for lifelong learning and acquiring new skills, enhancing employability and furthering personal and community growth.

With its ability to overcome geographical limitations, online teaching stands as a beacon of opportunity for remote and underserved communities, reaffirming the idea that education knows no bounds. It signifies a promising step toward a more inclusive and accessible educational landscape.

Enhances Equal Opportunities for Students with Disabilities

Online teaching serves as a beacon of hope for students living with disabilities, offering them numerous advantages that traditional in-person classes may not always provide. Let's delve deeper into how online education enriches the opportunities and experiences of students with disabilities:

- **Accessibility and Flexibility:** Traditional classroom settings often present unique challenges for students with disabilities, including physical barriers, difficulty accessing materials, or needing specialized accommodations. Online teaching bridges these gaps, allowing students to access course content and resources in ways that cater to their specific needs. Whether screen-reading software for visually impaired students or flexible scheduling for those with mobility impairments, online classes offer the adaptability required to ensure a comfortable and inclusive learning experience.

- **Individualized Learning:** Online teaching can adapt to the individual learning styles and preferences of students with disabilities. Instructors can provide alternative formats for course materials, such as audio versions for those with visual impairments, and offer additional support through interactive tools or captioning services. This personalization is pivotal in fostering every student's positive and successful educational journey.

- **Reduced Stigma and Stress:** Some students with disabilities may feel stigmatized or experience stress when attending traditional classes. Online teaching minimizes the social and environmental pressures often present in brick-and-mortar classrooms. This stress reduction contributes to a more relaxed and conducive learning atmosphere for students with disabilities, allowing them to focus on their studies and succeed.

- **Inclusive Learning Environment:** The online classroom promotes an inclusive and welcoming environment. It encourages peer interaction and collaboration, enabling students with disabilities to feel like valued academic community members. Inclusivity not only benefits students with disabilities but enriches the overall learning experience for all participants.

- **Improved Access to Resources:** Online teaching often offers a wealth of digital resources that can be easily customized to meet the needs of students with disabilities. These resources can include interactive simulations, alternative texts, and multimedia content with captioning. The digital format allows students to access and engage with resources more effectively.

- **Remote Support Services:** Online teaching seamlessly integrates support services for students with disabilities. These services may include accessible counseling, tutoring, or assistive technology training. Students can access these services remotely, ensuring they receive the necessary support for their academic and personal development.

- **Preparing for a Digital World:** In today's digital age, technological proficiency is an invaluable skill. Online teaching equips students with disabilities to navigate digital tools and platforms effectively, enhancing their preparedness for future academic and professional pursuits.

- **Empowering Independence:** Online teaching empowers students with disabilities to take charge of their education. They can manage their schedules, tailor their learning environments, and advocate for their unique needs. This sense of independence is a crucial component of personal growth and self-determination.

Online teaching breaks down barriers to education and fosters a more inclusive and accessible learning landscape. It ensures that every student, regardless of their challenges, can embark on a rewarding educational journey with the same opportunities for success.

Online teaching not only benefits students with disabilities but also plays a pivotal role in fostering a more equitable educational environment. Here are some additional points to highlight the significance of online teaching in enhancing equal opportunities, especially for students with disabilities:

- **Customized Learning Paths:** Online teaching allows for personalized learning paths tailored to individual students' needs. Students with disabilities can access materials in formats that best suit their requirements, ensuring the educational content is accessible to all. Customization is key to addressing diverse learning needs, whether it's enlarged text, audio transcripts, or interactive content.

- **Enhanced Communication:** Online teaching platforms often incorporate a range of communication tools, such as real-time chat, discussion forums, and video conferencing. These features facilitate communication between students and instructors, ensuring that students with disabilities can easily seek clarifications, engage in class discussions, and receive timely feedback on their progress.

- **Wider Resource Accessibility:** Digital resources and online teaching materials can be available in various formats. This enhances accessibility for disabled students who may require screen readers, text-to-speech software, or other assistive technologies. These tools enable all students to access and engage with course content effectively.

- **Accommodating Diverse Disabilities:** Online teaching is flexible and adaptable, accommodating various disabilities, from visual and auditory impairments to mobility challenges. Instructors can make use of features like closed captions, alt text for images, and keyboard shortcuts to ensure content is accessible to everyone.

- **Equitable Evaluation and Assessment:** Online teaching platforms often provide opportunities for varied assessment methods, ensuring that students with disabilities are assessed fairly. Instructors can use different formats for quizzes, assignments, and exams, allowing students to demonstrate their knowledge and skills in ways that align with their abilities.

- **Global Reach for Specialized Expertise:** Online teaching allows students with disabilities to access courses and expertise from around the world. This means they can benefit from specialized instructors and resources that may not be available in their local area. It broadens horizons and offers opportunities that were previously limited by geographical constraints.

- **Community and Support Networks:** Online teaching fosters virtual communities and support networks. Students with disabilities can connect with peers facing similar challenges, share experiences, and offer mutual support. Instructors can also provide additional guidance and resources for addressing specific needs.

In many ways, online teaching is a powerful tool for creating an inclusive, accommodating, and empowering educational environment for students with disabilities. Addressing unique challenges and providing equal opportunities paves the way for an education that embraces diversity and celebrates individual strengths.

Contributes to Digital Literacy

Another advantage of online learning is that it has contributed to developing digital literacy skills required in contemporary society and workplaces among students and teachers. This has helped teachers streamline some administrative aspects of teaching.

Can be Customized

We've mentioned how flexibility can help one set one's own study pace. However, online education is also flexible for each student's individual requirements and level of ability. Online classes tend to be smaller than conventional class sizes.

Generally, online learning platforms only allow one student at a time, and in almost all cases, this allows for greater interaction and more feedback between student and tutor.

One advantage of online learning is it can connect students and teachers worldwide. With traditional education, location dictates which classes one could sign up for. This isn't the case with online learning. One can sign up for classes all over the world, providing a more in-depth understanding of the global industry and helping children build their network and develop an international mindset.

With all these advantages of online teaching/learning, there is no need for scepticism about the internet.

Adapting to Online Teaching and Learning

Some people might find it hard to face the notion of leaving behind the conventional classroom, especially if it is to face the vast space of the internet. An alternative approach to learning should be embraced in a rapidly changing world since the internet has proven valid and valuable for many students and people who are tied and have to get on with their daily lives.

Research has shown that about 30% of higher education students take at least one distance course. Online learning/teaching can be a sensible choice for students, teachers, teenagers, and adults. As a student, this can be a helpful learning method for sharpening skills in a complex subject or learning a new skill.

In a space as vast as the internet, there are infinite skills and subjects to teach and learn. A growing number of universities and higher education colleges offer online versions of their programs for various levels and disciplines. From music composition to quantum physics, there are options for every student.

Studying a program online is also a great option for getting an official certificate, diploma, or degree without physically setting foot on a university campus. Nowadays, people get certificates that help them succeed in their professional careers.

About 90% of students today think that online learning is equal to or better than the traditional classroom experience. Each student has unique needs, and they must assess their unique situation and decide according to their needs and goals whether to choose online or traditional education or a mix of the two. While online education is not for everyone, it's still a convenient option with virtually endless options for international students all over the world.

Qualitative online learning leads to new, different, or more relevant outcomes. As a teacher, you need to rethink the way you teach when you go online, not just moving your face-to-face learning over to an online version but redesigning the teaching to fit the requirements of online learners.

Teaching well online has many of the exact requirements as teaching well face-to-face: for instance, clear learning outcomes and assessments that test for the desired learning outcomes and differentiate between different levels of achievement. However, there are also different requirements because the context in which learners (and you as an instructor) work will differ.

Online learning allows teachers/facilitators to deliver content or information in ways that lead to better learning than through a one-hour or more lecture course. A good body of research shows that online students need to feel that the instructor is present online; that is, interacting with students in discussion forums, directing them to recent relevant articles or events, and responding promptly to questions.

Instructors should be experts in their subject matter who know more than the students; thus, their job is to ensure that they transfer that information or knowledge to the students as effectively as possible. They should focus on developing learners' skills and the ability to question, analyze, and apply information or knowledge; they must both guide and facilitate.

You can design online courses to teach in any way, but moving your class online allows you to rethink your teaching, perhaps to tackle some of the limitations of classroom teaching, and to renew your approach to teaching.

If you are considering going online, take the opportunity before you start teaching to consider how you'd really like to be teaching and whether this can be accommodated in an online environment. It's not a decision you have to make immediately, though.

The important point is to be open to doing things differently.

To make optimum use of the advantages the online environment offers, online instructors need to remember that active learning is one of the keys to success in the online classroom. Instructors should employ new techniques and technologies to ensure their courses make the best of the online medium.

Summary

Online teaching is an important tool in expanding access to education to a wider range of students. One of the main advantages of online teaching is that it allows students living in remote or rural areas to access educational resources and classes that would otherwise be unavailable to them.

This is particularly beneficial for students living in areas with a shortage of qualified teachers or limited educational facilities. Online teaching can also provide greater flexibility for students with disabilities, allowing them to learn at their own pace and schedule with the help of assistive technology.

It also allows for greater flexibility in terms of scheduling, which can be particularly beneficial for working students or those with other commitments that make it difficult to attend traditional in-person classes. This allows students to learn at their own pace and schedule, which can be a significant advantage for students with busy or unpredictable schedules.

Online teaching can also provide opportunities for students to learn from teachers and experts worldwide, giving them access to a diverse range of perspectives and expertise.

Importantly, online teaching can be more cost-effective than traditional in-person classes. With online classes, students do not need to travel to a physical location to attend class, which can save time and money. Moreover, it eliminates the need for costly classroom materials since all the materials and resources can be accessed online.

Chapter 2: New Trends in Education Technology

Historically, the education sector has been slow to embrace technological advancements. The transition from classroom to home learning during the pandemic introduced new and innovative approaches to teaching and education. Among these, online classes have emerged as a valuable solution, enabling continuity in teaching.

The pandemic compelled us to adopt distance learning, leading to the discovery of digital trends that seamlessly integrate with traditional, in-person instruction.

Staying updated on innovative educational technology trends has become imperative for modern educators. Embracing cutting-edge technology empowers teachers to elevate the learning experience and frees them from repetitive tasks, enabling them to focus on nurturing students' intellectual growth.

Benefits of Educational Technology

Technology is already an integral part of many students' daily lives. There is immense potential to leverage it to further their education. Modern learners no longer want to be passive recipients of information; they seek interactive and experiential learning. Moreover, educational technology offers a host of advantages in the classroom.

Empowering Educators

Educational technology empowers educators to connect with their students on a deeper level and deliver content interactively, fostering a more engaging and immersive learning environment. In essence, the current trends in educational technology help teachers align their teaching methods with their student's interests and preferences.

Accommodate Different Learning Styles

Firstly, it addresses the challenge of accommodating different learning styles among students. Recognizing that students have diverse learning preferences, technology becomes a valuable ally for educators in customizing their lessons to cater to individual needs. Visual learners, for instance, can create infographics to demonstrate their understanding of the subject. In contrast, auditory learners can engage with interactive audio materials, fostering a more personalized and engaging learning experience.

Fosters Collaboration

Secondly, educational technology fosters student collaboration, extending its benefits beyond the classroom walls. When group projects are assigned, technology equips students with the tools necessary for effective collaboration, thereby enhancing their teamwork skills. Teachers can easily track each student's contributions and analyze the group's collective effort, instilling a sense of accountability and cooperation among learners.

Strengthens Bonding

Furthermore, educational technology has significantly strengthened the bond between students and teachers. Online platforms facilitate seamless communication, enabling students to share their ideas, participate actively in discussions, and engage in chats with their educators. According to research, approximately 57% of teachers and facilitators agree that the internet has positively impacted students' ability to articulate their thoughts and express opinions, ultimately leading to more efficient and meaningful connections in the learning process.

Future Benefits

In addition to immediate benefits, integrating technology in the classroom prepares students for their future careers in a technology-driven world. Familiarity with educational technology gained during their academic journey can be seamlessly transferred to various work-oriented software and tools, making it easier for students to adapt to the demands of future workplaces.

Interactive Learning Environment

Moreover, educational technology creates an engaging and interactive learning environment. By leveraging computers, tablets, and interactive videos, lessons are transformed into dynamic experiences that capture students' interest and attention. This interactive nature of technology not only enhances students' participation but also aids in the retention of information as they actively immerse themselves in the learning process.

Embracing educational technology in the classroom brings numerous benefits, ranging from personalized learning experiences and enhanced collaboration to strengthened student-teacher connections and better preparation for future challenges.

By leveraging the power of technology, educators can create a more engaging, inclusive, and effective educational experience for their students, empowering them for success in the modern world. Harnessing the power of educational technology allows teachers to create a more engaging, inclusive, and effective learning environment for their students. The emerging trends in educational technology are centred around connectivity, versatility, and student-focused learning.

By incorporating these new tools in the classroom, educators can now create more effective and personalized learning experiences, optimizing information delivery for better retention. Consequently, traditional teaching methods have undergone a transformative process, evolving into a more engaging and immersive educational journey.

The latest trends in educational technology bring a much-needed breath of fresh air. Additionally, the use of augmented reality and immersive learning has become crucial to enhance the learning experience and foster an environment for growth in education.

Artificial Intelligence (AI) and the Internet of Things (IoT)

We have witnessed many emerging trends in educational technology, including the Internet of Things (IoT) and Artificial Intelligence (AI). These interactive technologies have revolutionized the learning experience, offering students more engaging and dynamic learning methods.

Additionally, AI has proven to be an invaluable tool for teachers, assisting them in adapting lessons in real-time to cater to individual student's needs. It has also optimized the learning environment, improved communication, and enhanced the efficiency and quality of lesson planning.

Here's how AI is assisting educators in delivering effective and engaging online instruction:

• **Personalized Learning Paths:** AI analyzes students' learning behaviors, preferences, and performance to tailor personalized learning paths. This ensures that each student receives content and activities aligned with their individual needs and learning pace.

• **Smart Content Creation**: AI-powered tools can generate customized educational content, including quizzes, assignments, and study materials, based on the curriculum and learning objectives.

• **Automated Grading:** AI algorithms can assess and grade assignments, quizzes, and exams, providing instant feedback to students. This saves educators time and allows them to focus on providing meaningful guidance.

• **Intelligent Tutoring:** AI-driven virtual tutors can engage in real-time conversations with students, answering questions, explaining concepts, and providing assistance outside of regular class hours.

• **Data-Driven Insights**: AI analyzes student performance data to identify trends, strengths, and areas that need improvement. Educators can use these insights to adapt their teaching strategies and customize interventions.

- **Adaptive Assessments:** AI-powered assessments adjust the difficulty level of questions based on students' responses, ensuring a more accurate assessment of their knowledge and skills.

- **Engagement Monitoring:** AI tracks students' engagement levels and participation in online classes, allowing educators to identify students who may need additional support or encouragement.

- **Language Translation:** AI tools can provide real-time translation of educational content and communications, making online teaching more inclusive for students from diverse language backgrounds.

- **Content Recommendations:** AI analyzes students' learning behaviors to recommend relevant resources, videos, and supplementary materials that align with their interests and learning goals.

- **Virtual Labs and Simulations:** AI-powered simulations and virtual labs provide hands-on experiences for students, enhancing their understanding of complex concepts and practical skills.

- **Early Intervention:** AI identifies struggling students based on their performance data and alerts educators, enabling timely interventions to provide targeted support.

•   **Interactive Learning:** AI-driven interactive elements, such as chatbots, quizzes, and interactive multimedia, make online lessons more engaging and interactive for students.

•   **Continuous Improvement:** By analyzing student interactions with content and activities, AI helps educators refine and improve their teaching methods over time.

•   **Feedback Enhancement:** AI tools can provide detailed feedback on students' assignments, highlighting areas of improvement in terms of content, grammar, and structure.

•   **Learner Analytics:** AI-generated analytics provide educators with insights into students' progress, engagement, and learning behaviors, enabling informed decision-making.

AI is, indeed, empowering online educators to deliver more personalized, effective, and engaging learning experiences. It frees up educators' time from administrative tasks, enabling them to focus on meaningful interactions with students and the continuous improvement of their teaching methods. As AI continues to evolve, it holds the potential to further enhance the online teaching environment and create a more enriching educational journey for both educators and learners.

In today's educational landscape, computers and the internet have become as prevalent as textbooks and pencils, presenting a significant opportunity to enhance students' performance.

By harnessing technology, educators can gain insights into each student's unique needs and create personalized learning solutions. Technology, such as auto-grading, can alleviate the burden on educators while providing a more interactive and engaging learning experience.

Furthermore, personalized learning pathways are becoming more prominent in educational technology. With the help of data analytics and AI, educational platforms can assess each student's strengths and weaknesses, interests, and learning preferences.

This information creates personalized learning pathways, tailoring the content and pace of instruction to suit each student's individual needs. This approach fosters a deeper understanding of the material and allows students to progress at their own pace, promoting a more effective and efficient learning experience.

Virtual Reality (VR) and Augmented Reality (AR) in Learning

Another notable trend in educational technology is the integration of Virtual Reality (VR) and Augmented Reality (AR) into the learning experience. VR immerses students in a computer-generated simulation, providing them with a 3D environment that mimics real-life scenarios. AR, on the other hand, overlays digital content in the real world, enhancing the learning experience by combining physical and virtual elements.

These technologies have immense potential in various subjects, from history and geography, where students can virtually explore historical sites and landmarks, to science and engineering, where they can interactively visualize complex concepts. VR and AR provide unparalleled engagement, making learning more enjoyable and effective.

AR and VR technologies offer interactive and immersive learning opportunities that engage students' senses and provide new and exciting experiences.

While VR creates a fully constructed virtual reality, AR enhances the real world by overlaying digital content, making lessons more approachable and enjoyable for students. Immersive learning allows students to explore environments, participate in experiments, and experience historical sites, bringing lessons to life and directly influencing student performance in the classroom.

Gamification of Learning

Gamification has emerged as a powerful tool in education. Gamification incorporates game-like elements, such as points, rewards, and challenges, into the learning process. Students become more motivated to participate actively and achieve learning objectives by turning lessons into games.

Gamified learning environments stimulate healthy competition, encourage problem-solving, and foster a sense of accomplishment, increasing students' interest and retention in the subject matter.

Educators are constantly seeking innovative ways to make learning enjoyable and engaging, and gamification has emerged as a promising solution. By applying game-like mechanics to daily activities, gamification increases student engagement and fosters a positive learning environment.

This trend has gained momentum in primary education, where students can acquire knowledge while feeling like they're participating in a fun and interactive game. Gamification not only enhances student engagement but also aids in their cognitive development and promotes collaboration among students.

Use of Social Media

The use of social media in education is also on the rise. Educational institutions and teachers are leveraging various social media platforms to facilitate communication, collaboration, and student engagement.

Social media provides an accessible and familiar medium for students to interact with their peers and educators, allowing for discussions, sharing of resources, and timely updates. Social media can enhance the learning experience and promote a positive learning community when used responsibly.

While I have often emphasized the negative aspects of social media, it's important to note that various types of social media platforms play a crucial role in enhancing online learning experiences. These platforms offer a range of benefits, including:

• **Discussion Forums and Online Communities:** Platforms like Reddit, Stack Overflow, and Quora provide learners with spaces to ask questions, share insights, and engage in conversations related to specific topics. Online communities dedicated to education enable users to seek help, share knowledge, and connect with like-minded individuals.

• **Social Networking Platforms:** General social networking platforms like Facebook and LinkedIn host groups and pages dedicated to educational topics. Learners can participate in discussions, access resources, and connect with peers and professionals in their field.

- **Microblogging Platforms:** Twitter is widely used in education to share bite-sized information, resources, and insights. Educators and institutions utilize hashtags to curate discussions around specific topics, enabling learners to follow relevant content.

- **Professional Networking:** LinkedIn is a valuable platform for online learning, connecting learners with professionals, experts, and industry leaders. Users can join groups, engage in discussions, and access articles and posts related to their field of interest.

- **Video Sharing Platforms:** YouTube and Vimeo offer educational channels and content, ranging from tutorials and lectures to demonstrations and documentaries. These platforms cater to diverse learning styles and provide engaging visual and auditory experiences.

- **Podcasting Platforms:** Podcasts are increasingly popular for mobile learning. Apple Podcasts and Spotify host educational podcasts covering a wide array of subjects, offering flexible learning options.

- **Collaboration Tools:** Google Workspace (formerly G Suite) and Microsoft Teams provide collaborative features like document sharing, real-time editing, and video conferencing. These tools facilitate group projects and virtual teamwork.

- **Blogging Platforms:** Educators share in-depth articles, tutorials, and insights on platforms like WordPress and Medium. Learners can access these resources to gain a deeper understanding of complex topics.

- **Virtual Classrooms and Learning Management Systems (LMS):** While not traditional social media, virtual classrooms and LMS platforms like Moodle and Blackboard provide spaces for instructors and students to interact, share resources, submit assignments, and engage in discussions. These dedicated online learning platforms have integrated social features that allow learners to engage with instructors and peers, ask questions, and participate in discussion boards related to specific courses.

- **Specialized Platforms:** Platforms like Edmodo and Schoology are designed specifically for education, offering features tailored to educators, students, and parents for effective communication and collaboration.

These platforms offer tools and features that foster communication, collaboration, and engagement among learners and educators. In conclusion, social media has revolutionized online learning by promoting active engagement, facilitating collaboration, and making learning resources more accessible and personalized. Its seamless integration with education platforms empowers educators and learners to create vibrant virtual learning communities that transcend traditional boundaries.

Mobile Learning

Additionally, the shift towards mobile learning or m-learning has been gaining momentum. As mobile devices become increasingly prevalent, educational content and applications are being optimized for smartphones and tablets. M-learning enables students to access learning materials anytime, anywhere, promoting flexible and self-directed learning. Mobile apps and platforms offer various educational resources, from interactive quizzes and language learning tools to virtual libraries and study guides.

Cloud Technology in Education

Cloud technology software has proven invaluable in fostering collaboration among students and simplifying their access to educational resources. Its popularity soared during school shutdowns, and it continues to thrive even with in-person learning restored. With cloud technology, students can collaborate on projects and access programs and files from any device, be it a laptop, desktop, tablet, or phone. It also offers expanded access to STEAM (Science, Technology, Engineering, Arts, and Mathematics) programs, contributing to a more enriched and holistic learning experience while saving teachers valuable time on computer updates.

Asynchronous Online Learning

Asynchronous online learning has given students greater flexibility and freedom during school. This approach empowers students to set their preferred learning schedule within a given timeframe. They can access instructional materials at any time during the week, provided they complete their required assignments and tasks.

Asynchronous learning encourages students to actively participate in their education, developing self-sufficiency and time-management skills. The flexibility of online learning allows students to access materials from any location, further supporting their personalized learning journey.

In today's digital learning environment, various educational technologies have become essential tools for students and teachers. These advanced systems offer a more environmentally friendly approach by reducing paper waste.

Some of the vital educational technology devices include projectors, which facilitate the projection of notes, images, or presentations onto flat surfaces; smartboards, which enable digitization and capturing written content; laptops and tablets, versatile electronic devices for typing notes and engaging in online learning activities; and ultra-high-definition televisions, ideal for showing educational movies and video displays on wide-screen TVs. It's crucial to ensure these devices' proper storage and charging to maintain their longevity and usability.

As educational technology continues to evolve, embracing these trends and incorporating the latest tools and methods will significantly enhance the learning experience, empowering students to thrive and succeed in an ever-changing digital world

Summary

Historically, the education sector has been slow to embrace technology trends and has undergone a refreshing change with the latest educational technology advancements. The pandemic's impact accelerated the adoption of these trends, ushering in new education methods. Online classes, augmented reality, immersive learning, and other innovative technologies have emerged, offering fresh opportunities to address the growing needs of education.

Educational technology provides a personalized and immersive learning experience while assisting educators in delivering information effectively and tailoring solutions for individual students.

Auto-grading technology lightens the burden on educators and enhances the learning experience for students. Moreover, educational technology's integration of diverse learning styles caters to students' needs, fostering a more inclusive educational environment.

The collaborative potential of educational technology empowers students to work together, both inside and outside the classroom, fostering teamwork and cooperation. Teachers can effectively track contributions and analyze collective efforts to nurture an engaging learning community.

The student-teacher connection has been significantly strengthened through the impact of the internet, enabling efficient online discussions and chats that promote better communication and understanding.

Integrating technology in the classroom equips students with valuable skills for the future job market, where technology plays an increasingly pivotal role. Familiarity with technology gained in an educational setting prepares students to comfortably adapt to work-oriented software and technological workflows.

In conclusion, the education sector is finally catching up with technology trends, and educational technology is transforming the learning landscape. It delivers personalized learning experiences, supports educators in their roles, enhances collaboration and communication, and prepares students for future success.

To provide the best possible education for students, educators and institutions must remain informed about the latest trends and developments in educational technology. By embracing these advancements, educators can create an engaging, inclusive, and effective educational experience, empowering students for a bright and successful future in the digital age.

Chapter 3: The Secret of Every Top Instructor

Instructors play a pivotal role in shaping their students' lives by imparting knowledge and essential skills for their future careers. Whether in schools, colleges, universities, or online learning platforms, teachers are expected to possess various qualities, such as innovation, patience, knowledge, professionalism, and confidence.

These inspiring traits include subject expertise, a sense of humor, and effective teaching methods. Being approachable and avoiding aggression or arrogance are essential for creating a positive learning environment for the students.

An instructor's role is vital in driving the educational system within every educational institution. A great instructor engages with learners, demonstrates understanding, and embodies various virtues to become the best in their field. Teachers are integral members of society, and many successful professionals owe their achievements to the guidance of instructors during their academic journey.

The foundation of any subject is firmly laid in educational institutions, making teachers key contributors to students' growth. As role models and sources of inspiration, effective teachers offer numerous benefits to students, such as thought-provoking environments, structured learning, constructive feedback, tailored education, and opportunities for hands-on training and teamwork.

Qualities of a Great Teacher

Effective teachers possess essential characteristics, including preparedness, creativity, resourcefulness, impartiality, a positive attitude, compassion, and a lifelong commitment to learning. The definition of effective instruction encompasses various aspects, such as teacher behavior, warmth, clarity, knowledge of the subject matter, and alignment with students' and teachers' beliefs.

Resource Specialists

Instructors should act as resource specialists, knowledgeable in finding information and guiding students or co-workers on how to use it effectively. They must support and encourage students to learn new skills or handle information, take on roles like coaching, leading, and counseling, and even assist other teachers in their professional circles.

Mentor

Mentorship is another significant role that teachers or instructors can assume. Learners look up to instructors as role models and may emulate their behavior and work ethic. Experienced teachers can mentor their younger colleagues entering the profession, offering guidance and support.

Lifelong Learner

Being a lifelong learner is an essential quality for effective instructors. Sharing knowledge and experiences is crucial, as there is always something new to learn every day in teaching or training. As learners themselves, teachers continue to grow and develop, continuously improving as professionals. Embracing opportunities for personal and professional growth is vital for aspiring teachers, and teachers dedicated to their subjects with a passion for learning make the most impactful educators.

Tolerance

Cultural tolerance and appreciation for diversity are traits of good and effective instructors, fostering a calm, tolerant, and friendly classroom environment. Effective teachers help students reach their fullest potential in learning by motivating students through their professional and personal skills.

Superior Subject Knowledge

Possessing superior subject knowledge, enthusiasm, and communication skills are enviable features of a good teacher. The ability to explain complex concepts using simple language is crucial to becoming a great instructor.

Communicate Effectively and Listen Actively

Effective communication is a must for teachers, as it creates a positive and comfortable learning atmosphere, encourages feedback, and facilitates positive engagement with the subject. Listening is equally vital, as skilled teachers can pick up on unspoken anxieties and adapt their teaching to suit students' individual needs. Teachers can better understand their students and tailor their lessons by listening well.

Foster Collaboration and Flexibility

Collaboration is a cornerstone of effective teaching. Teachers often work in groups, requiring flexibility, effort, and commitment to work harmoniously together. Collaboration involves sharing expectations, involving co-workers in planning, appreciating diverse personalities, and demonstrating a positive attitude towards teamwork. Effective collaboration results in reduced stress, increased enjoyment, and greater benefits for both educators and students

Being Adaptable

In an ever-changing world, adaptability is a crucial skill for effective teachers. Working in a constantly evolving environment requires adjusting teaching methods based on students' understanding, available resources, curriculum, practices, and requirements. Staying informed about trends, standards, and new research is essential for continual improvement. Reading your audience and adapting your teaching style to suit their needs is a hallmark of an engaging teacher.

Engage Students

Engaging students involves humor, creativity, and a strong classroom presence. It goes beyond passive lecturing and requires active participation in the learning process. Engaging with the class enables teachers to know their students better, pace lessons effectively, set clear expectations, incorporate active and varied learning experiences, and demonstrate care for students' development.

Being Empathetic

A caring and empathetic ethos lies at the heart of purposeful teaching. Understanding students' logical and emotional behaviors, mental evolution, and motivation levels is key to selecting effective teaching methods. Empathy plays a significant role in connecting with students and improving their learning experiences. Treating each student as an individual and being attentive and understanding of their circumstances fosters meaningful connections and positively impacts their learning journey.

Having Patience

Patience is a virtue that distinguishes great teachers. They never give up on their students and explore new ways to help them succeed. Classroom management, working with diverse colleagues, and addressing student issues require patience and thoughtful approaches. Focusing on prior knowledge and assessing students' readiness for new learning demonstrates patience in building a strong foundation for their development.

In challenging situations, such as dealing with disruptive behavior or supporting students with learning disabilities, exercising patience is essential. Teachers' patience levels can influence students' self-confidence and performance. Demonstrating positivity and encouragement can have a transformative impact on students' self-esteem and academic achievements.

As educators, teachers have the power to make a positive difference in their students' lives. They create a conducive and supportive learning environment that nurtures students' growth and development by cultivating adaptability, engagement, empathy, and patience.

These qualities are the secret to becoming exceptional instructors who inspire and guide their students toward success and personal fulfilment.

The Four Secrets of Every Top Instructor

Instructors play a pivotal role in shaping students' lives by imparting knowledge and skills essential for their personal and professional growth.

Becoming a top instructor involves embracing four key secrets that elevate the teaching experience and inspire a love for learning among students.

Secret 1: To Love to Learn

The first secret is to love to learn, a state characterized by a genuine interest and passion for acquiring new knowledge and understanding. Top instructors embody this attitude by being active and engaged learners themselves. They lead by example, sharing their own joy and satisfaction in discovering new things.

Creating an engaging and interactive learning environment encourages students' curiosity and exploration. By providing opportunities for student choice and celebrating effort and progress, they foster a growth mindset that sees challenges as opportunities for growth.

Secret 2: To Love to Share the Knowledge that You Have Accumulated

The second secret is to love to share the knowledge that instructors have accumulated. This involves a genuine interest in helping others learn and grow. Top instructors are passionate about their subject matter and enjoy mentoring and coaching others. They create an open and approachable environment, encouraging students to ask questions and seek help.

Sharing personal experiences and real-world connections makes learning relatable and meaningful. Providing resources and acting as mentors empowers students to take charge of their learning journey. Top instructors share their expertise outside the classroom through public speaking, writing, and professional development, enriching the wider educational community.

These two secrets intertwine to form the foundation of effective teaching and student engagement. By loving to learn and sharing that knowledge, top instructors inspire a love for learning in their students.

Secret 3: To Love to Connect with Students

Instructors who embrace the third secret are able to foster strong bonds with their students. They demonstrate empathy and understanding, considering each student's unique needs and backgrounds. Being attentive and compassionate creates a safe and supportive learning environment, allowing students to thrive academically and emotionally.

Listening actively and observing closely, they pick up on students' anxieties and challenges, providing the necessary support and encouragement.

Secret 4: To Embrace Adaptability and Openness to Change

Finally, top instructors are adaptable and open to change. They understand that the world of education is constantly evolving, and they must adjust their teaching methods accordingly.

Being willing to learn from their students and colleagues, they stay informed about new trends and research. Their ability to adapt to students' understanding, available resources, and curriculum requirements ensures they remain effective educators despite changing circumstances.

In conclusion, every top instructor embraces four secrets that define their excellence. They love to learn and share their knowledge, fostering a culture of curiosity and growth. They connect with their students, creating a nurturing and supportive learning environment. Furthermore, they remain adaptable and open to change, ensuring their teaching remains relevant and impactful. By incorporating these secrets, instructors can elevate their teaching practice and inspire a love for learning in their students.

Summary

Building a strong foundation of knowledge and real-world experience is critical to becoming a great instructor or teacher. No matter where your career path takes you in the education sector, your teaching can profoundly impact students' lives, and your education is the foundation for that work.

Teachers or instructors can make such a huge impact on their students' lives. Being a teacher is an extraordinary gift, and those who have that gift make a positive, lasting impression on the lives of their students that can change the trajectory of their lives.

Some of the most desirable traits and qualities of effective great teachers or instructors are subject knowledge, communication skills, and a sense of humor. Being partial and aggressive are negative qualities that can signpost you as an incompetent teacher. Teachers must possess positive qualities and shun negative traits to create a better learning environment.

Other characteristics of effective teaching include an engaging classroom presence, value in real-world learning, exchange of best practices, listening, collaboration, adaptability, empathy, patience, and a lifelong love of learning.

A good teacher can make a world of difference in a student's life, impacting everything from classroom learning to long-term success. They play a vital role in the education system by providing students with the knowledge and skills necessary for their future careers and lives.

They are responsible for creating a positive and supportive learning environment and for being patient and understanding of their student's unique learning needs and challenges.

One of the most essential characteristics of a top instructor is a genuine love for learning. This involves having a passion for acquiring new knowledge and skills and being excited about the potential to grow and develop professionally. This enthusiasm for learning is contagious and can inspire students to create their own love for learning.

Another crucial characteristic of a top instructor is a love for sharing the knowledge that they have accumulated. This involves recognizing the value of their knowledge and experience and sharing it with others. This can take the form of providing students with the resources, materials, and opportunities to learn and grow and sharing personal experiences and anecdotes to help students understand and relate to the subject matter.

Being kind to students is another critical aspect of being a top instructor. This involves creating a positive and supportive learning environment, being patient and understanding of students' needs, and being willing to go the extra mile to help them succeed. This includes recognizing that students come from diverse backgrounds and have different learning styles and experiences and trying to be inclusive and culturally responsive.

Being mindful to give positive energy to learners is also vital. This involves being aware and intentional about the energy and atmosphere you create in the classroom and making adjustments as needed to create a positive and supportive environment that fosters learning and encourages students to be engaged and motivated.

A great instructor is also resourceful, a mentor, and a lifelong learner. They should be approachable, patient, knowledgeable, and professional. They should be a great listener, resourceful and supportive, have a sense of humor and a positive attitude, and possess creativity, impartiality, and compassion.

They should also be able to adapt to individual students' needs. Being a mentor, they can guide and support the students in their learning journey.

Chapter 4: Finding Your PCR (Passion, Commitment, and Resilience)

According to Merriam-Webster, *'passion'* refers to a strong feeling of enthusiasm or excitement for or about doing something.

Passions often relate to things you would love to do constantly. Sometimes passion can be something you like to do for work. Passion for your work is more specific than being excited or enthusiastic about something.

As a passionate person, you will always be motivated to dig into tough problems and through different challenges and setbacks in your duty. This will bring out your desire to figure something out, learn faster, and make an impact.

It is essential to understand that there is a difference between passion and core values. Core values shape how you will feel about your work or work environment. Some strong core values might include discipline, perseverance, playfulness, learning, excellence, commitment, and resilience.

Passion is what sets you apart from others who teach online. Your pre-existing passion for serving as an online instructor distinguishes you.

Essentially, passion serves as a potent force that propels you beyond the ordinary, especially within the realm of online education. This very passion infuses innovation, differentiates your endeavors, and elevates standard teaching into an extraordinary experience. As you embark on your journey of online instruction, remember that your passion acts as the catalyst positioning you for success, forming the bedrock for remarkable accomplishments and contributions.

Why Should You Find Your Passion?

Pursuing your passion amplifies your care for your work, emotions, and intellectual engagement. The desire to engage in your job grows stronger, even in the face of challenges. This direct connection between uncovering and nurturing your passions is intricately tied to your career and personal development growth.

The stronger one's passion is for their job, the more motivated they are to invest in self-improvement, significantly enhancing their likelihood of success.

Passion transcends mere excitement; it evolves into a devoted commitment to your craft. The fire in your belly distinguishes you from others, setting you apart as someone not only enthusiastic but also deeply devoted to your work. As an online instructor, your passion serves as the driving force, propelling you to tackle intricate problems and endure setbacks.

As you harness your passion for online instruction, you're not merely disseminating information but sharing a piece of your essence. This ardor radiates through your courses, captivating learners and inspiring them to embark on their personal, educational journeys. Your unwavering dedication sets you apart in the expansive realm of online educators, making you a beacon of inspiration for those eager to learn and grow.

In online education, passion is the key that unlocks doors, fuels innovation, and metamorphoses ordinary courses into extraordinary experiences. The driving force compels you to strive for excellence, ensuring your influence is long-lasting. So, as you embark on the path of crafting, marketing, and teaching online courses, remember that passion acts as the wind beneath your wings, propelling you to fresh pinnacles of success and fulfilment.

Success and Passion

Success is defined as the achievement of a desired aim or purpose. Many people think that success involves amassing wealth or achieving a certain level of fame, but the true success that satisfies is not all about money.

Success means that you are proud of accomplishing your set goals and objectives and being part of something that matters to you. The thirst for success inspires people to work hard, be loyal, and get involved in teamwork. Success without significance, purpose, service, and meaningful relationships is not possible.

No matter how difficult a course of business or a job might be, passion can fuel and drive people toward their specific goals. When people have a passion for what they do, they will have strong values, persistence, talent, and intellect, eventually contributing to success. Passionate people are enthusiastic and can easily plow through the biggest obstacles and overcome the most intractable challenges. Passion helps people to be more resilient when encountering obstacles, to solve problems easily, and to have a more positive outlook.

How to Find Your Passion

To find your passion, you should create a personal vision statement, determine your values, find your true north, list the things you love to do, assess the things you don't love, acknowledge your strengths and achievements, practice journaling, embrace a mindfulness practice, seek guidance from a coach, and surround yourself with people with similar passions.

Seeking out other successful people and mentors in your area of passion can help you see how they are operating and making their decisions. By integrating these practices into your life, you can uncover your passions and enhance your journey up the professional ladder while nurturing a strong sense of self-worth.

Following Your Passion

Following your passion does not necessarily mean that you can be successful. Passion relies on other different factors for success to happen. Passionate people follow what interests them and are always excited about it. They never feel tired or pressured in the work environment.

Pursuing a career without getting the expected results or outcome can damage a person's mindset. This can lead to poor judgments and decision-making capabilities and to hating what they thought was their passion. Once you have decided on your passion, adopt the perspective that you can do what you love. Strengthening this belief is to surround yourself with people with whom you share your point of view.

Commitment

Commitment is the devotion, trust, and loyalty given to an individual, a company, or an organization, and it is an important element since it positively influences organizational effectiveness and employees' well-being. It is the willingness and a strong determination to strive to perform the task and to obey all rules with consciousness and a full sense of responsibility.

In the realm of online courses, commitment is multifaceted. For creators, it entails a profound willingness to invest time, effort, and expertise in developing course content that resonates with learners. This commitment goes beyond the mere creation of content; it involves a conscientious understanding of learners' needs and aspirations. Creators who approach their work with dedication and a sense of responsibility are more likely to craft courses that engage, inspire, and empower students.

Likewise, commitment influences the selling of online courses. When course providers demonstrate a genuine commitment to the value and impact of their offerings, potential learners are more likely to trust the authenticity and relevance of the content. The commitment to delivering tangible benefits and enriching the lives of students can create a strong bond of trust, ultimately driving course enrolment and fostering a positive reputation.

Moreover, commitment plays a crucial role in the teaching aspect of online courses. Instructors who approach their teaching role with devotion and a full sense of responsibility create a dynamic learning environment. Learners can sense when educators are genuinely invested in their progress, which enhances their motivation and engagement. This commitment involves conveying knowledge effectively and providing timely feedback, addressing queries, and guiding students on their learning journey.

In the broader perspective, commitment is not merely about following rules and completing tasks; it's about embodying a strong determination to excel and contribute meaningfully.

As the online education landscape evolves, individuals and organizations prioritizing commitment are better positioned to navigate challenges, adapt to changing dynamics, and create lasting impacts. By fostering commitment, whether in course creation, sales, or instruction, a holistic approach is taken to ensure the growth of both the educational ecosystem and the individuals within it.

Commitment and Leadership

Commitment can affect someone's job performance. A person not committed to their role can never be a leader. Institutional performance increases when employees are committed to a certain course of the organization. This is a key factor in the success of any organization, as it is directly linked to employee engagement, productivity, and job satisfaction.

Commitment plays a crucial role in employee retention. When employees are committed to their work, they are more likely to put in extra effort, be more engaged in their tasks, shun absenteeism, and be less likely to leave the company. This can save the company money and resources that would otherwise be spent on hiring and training new employees.

Leadership is also closely linked to commitment. A person not committed to their work is unlikely to be a successful leader, as they will not have the drive and determination needed to inspire others to follow their lead. However, a leader who is fully committed to their work is more likely to be able to motivate and inspire others to be committed.

Commitment takes various forms, including a willingness to exceed assigned duties, a deep sense of loyalty to the company, and a fervent desire to witness the company's success. It also encompasses the readiness to undertake extra responsibilities and additional tasks when required.

For example, a committed educator will develop leadership skills and might go beyond the core curriculum to ensure learners acquire a comprehensive understanding, thereby enhancing the overall learning experience. Commitment is the adhesive that binds innovation, leadership, and success throughout the journey of creating, selling, and teaching online courses.

It empowers leaders to inspire and rally others, fosters employee trust and loyalty, and establishes a solid foundation for sustained growth. The pursuit of commitment is not merely a task; it's a transformative journey that elevates the trajectory of online education, propelling creators, sellers, and instructors to reach new pinnacles of excellence.

Resilience

Resilience is a complex and multidimensional construct that refers to the capacity of individuals, communities, and systems to adapt and recover from adversity, stress, or change. It can be viewed as a dynamic process involving coping, adapting, and recovering from difficult situations.

There are three forms of resilience, namely:

- **Individual resilience:** It refers to the ability of a person to cope with stress and adversity and change healthily and adaptively. This can include regulating emotions, maintaining positive relationships, and engaging in problem-solving and decision-making.

- **Community resilience:** This refers to the ability of a group of people to come together and support one another in times of stress or adversity. This can include things like strong social connections, access to resources, and effective communication.

- **System resilience:** This refers to a system's ability, such as organizations or societies, to adapt and recover from disruption or change. This can include effective crisis management, flexible infrastructure, and clear lines of communication.

Various factors, such as genetics, early childhood experiences, social support, and access to resources, can influence resilience. It can also be developed and strengthened through intentional practices such as mindfulness, cognitive-behavioral therapy, and community-building activities.

How Resilience Can Help with Online Teaching

Along with passion and commitment, resilience is also an integral trait in online teaching because it helps educators navigate the challenges and uncertainty of teaching in a virtual environment.

The following are some specific ways resilience can be important for online teaching.

- **Adapting to change:** Online teaching often requires educators to quickly adapt to new technologies, teaching methods, and student needs. Resilience can help educators remain flexible and open to new ideas, making it easier to adjust to changes.

- **Coping with technical difficulties:** Technical issues are common in online teaching, and educators need to be able to deal with these and find solutions quickly. Resilience can help educators maintain a positive attitude and not get discouraged in such situations.

- **Maintaining student engagement:** Online teaching can be more challenging than in-person teaching when keeping students engaged. Resilience can help educators devise creative ways to maintain student engagement, even when faced with technical difficulties or student apathy.

- **Managing stress:** Online teaching can be stressful, especially when dealing with uncertainty and isolation. Resilience can help educators manage stress, maintain a positive attitude, and focus on their goals.

- **Building relationships:** Online teaching can be more isolating than in-person teaching, and it can be harder to build relationships with students. Resilience can help educators intentionally build relationships and create a positive learning environment, even when working remotely.

Leading a classroom online is challenging and requires resilience to overcome the lack of physical presence, build trust, and maintain authority. Overall, resilience can help online educators deal with the unique challenges of teaching in a virtual environment and provide a better learning experience for their students.

Summary

In today's competitive world of online education, the importance of Passion, Commitment, and Resilience (PCR) cannot be overstated. These three elements are foundational pillars for educators and institutions seeking to provide high-quality and impactful virtual learning experiences.

Passion ignites the spark within educators, pushing them to explore innovative teaching methods and connect with their students on a profound level. It's the force that transforms ordinary courses into extraordinary ones. When educators are passionate about their subjects and their role in shaping their students' futures, it translates into engaging, inspiring, and empowering learning experiences. This passion sets dedicated educators apart in the vast landscape of online education.

However, passion alone is not enough to ensure sustained success. Commitment is equally critical in ensuring the authenticity and relevance of educational content. It involves a deep dedication to developing course materials that resonate with students. It's a commitment to understanding students' needs and aspirations, creating trust, and ultimately driving enrollment. Commitment extends to teaching, where instructors create dynamic learning environments by delivering knowledge effectively, providing timely feedback, and guiding students on their educational journeys.

In a broader context, commitment is about fostering a strong determination to excel and contribute meaningfully. It is a transformative journey that elevates online education, benefiting both learners and educators.

Resilience is the third component of PCR and plays a vital role in online education. It enables educators to navigate the challenges and uncertainties inherent in virtual teaching. Resilience helps educators adapt to technological changes, cope with technical difficulties, maintain student engagement, manage stress, and build strong student–teacher relationships. With resilience, educators can thrive in the virtual teaching environment, providing a better learning experience for their students.

In summary, Passion, Commitment, and Resilience (PCR) are the cornerstones of success in online education. They empower educators and institutions to meet the unique demands of virtual teaching, create outstanding learning experiences, and drive positive impacts. As the world of online education continues to evolve, embracing PCR is the key to achieving new levels of excellence and innovation.

Chapter 5: Things to Know Before You Create Your First Online Course

Creating and selling online courses has become increasingly popular in response to the growing demand for online education and the opportunity to generate income. However, before diving into this venture, it's essential to understand what it takes to develop a successful online course. This process involves selecting the right subject matter, testing your ideas, conducting thorough research, crafting a course outline, creating course content, launching your course online, marketing it effectively, collecting feedback, and fostering a learning community.

Imparting knowledge and expertise through an online course offers a unique avenue to establish yourself as an authority in your field, foster a community of like-minded individuals around your business, and expand your influence—all from the convenience of your own home. From selecting the optimal subject matter to cultivating a thriving learning community, let's explore these essential steps in detail.

Identify Your Target Audience

Before getting started, it's crucial to identify your target audience and assess the demand for your chosen topic. Seek input from friends, colleagues, and your existing audience regarding their interest in the subject matter you have in mind. This initial step allows you to better tailor your course content and marketing efforts to those who will find it most valuable.

Understanding your audience's preferences, preferred content formats, and current knowledge levels will help you create a more focused and effective course.

Choose the Right Subject

Selecting the appropriate subject matter is a fundamental decision that significantly influences the success of your online course. The key criterion for evaluating your topic is its appeal to both you and your audience. To effectively educate students, instructors need a deep understanding of the subject matter, enabling them to help learners create mental frameworks, connect ideas, and address misconceptions.

Your chosen topic should either be an area in which you are already knowledgeable or one that you are willing to thoroughly explore. Passion for the subject is essential. Consider your areas of expertise and what topics people frequently seek your advice on, as these often make successful online courses. Alternatively, choose a subject you're eager to learn about, as your own learning journey can enhance your teaching.

Conduct online research to identify topics that are in demand. The existence of competition in the form of other online courses can be a positive sign, indicating that people find the subject relevant and beneficial. Creating content that complements existing offerings can also be a strategic approach.

Understand the Challenges

Effective teaching requires instructors to connect concepts across their field and relate them to real-world applications. This foundational understanding forms the basis of pedagogical content knowledge, enabling you to convey ideas effectively to others.

Investigate the impact of your teaching on student learning and keep up with educational research to adapt to diverse learning needs. Training in analysis helps you view the world from multiple perspectives and better serve a variety of learners.

Investing in Hardware

Creating an engaging online course necessitates specific tools and resources, though some may be optional, and alternatives with built-in features are available. A desktop or laptop is essential for course content creation and delivery, while a microphone is necessary for recording lectures and tutorials. A camera, whether on a smartphone or a dedicated device, is required for recording videos or providing visual aids.

Fortunately, a high-quality online course can be created with relatively simple equipment. Your expertise and the quality of education you provide are paramount, allowing you to produce valuable content from your home.

Various approaches are viable options, such as speaking directly to the camera, recording your screen, or conducting live classes. If you choose to record yourself, you'll also need to handle video editing.

Additional tools, such as a flip chart with a stand, a whiteboard, paper, and markers, can enhance the course with visual aids, diagrams, and illustrations. Access to a desktop, laptop, tablet, or smartphone with internet connectivity is essential for students. Headphones with a microphone improve audio quality during virtual classes and reduce background noise.

Both instructors and students benefit from having a notebook and pen for note-taking and idea-jotting. These tools contribute to a successful and enriching online learning experience. Some courses may have specific technical requirements, such as a particular web browser or software version, which learners should be aware of.

Testing Out the Idea

Creating an online course is a substantial undertaking, so testing your concept before diving in is wise. Begin by creating a landing page for your upcoming course with a concise description of what participants can expect to learn and compelling imagery reflecting the course's essence.

Test your concept by utilizing polls or online forms to gauge your audience's interest. Create a short tutorial to monitor its performance, and then solicit feedback through social media and other platforms to determine if there is substantial interest.

You can invite visitors to sign up for a free preview of your course or offer pre-purchase options to reserve a spot. After promoting your website through various channels, analyze the data you collect to gauge interest and gather feedback.

Track Progress and Research Further

Define metrics in advance to measure the success of your course during the trial period. Consider offering a free mini-course derived from specific sections or concepts of the main course to give potential students a risk-free taste of what you offer.

As your course gains traction, conduct further research on your chosen topic. Whether you are an expert or a learner, in-depth research helps you provide more comprehensive content than what is readily available. Explore various sources, including literature, competitor courses, libraries, and webinars, and conduct keyword research to understand your audience's interests.

Going the extra mile in research allows you to offer unique angles and expand the scope of your course, adding significant value to your students.

Developing a Course Outline

After thorough research, create a comprehensive course outline. Break down your lessons into main topics, ensuring a logical progression from one idea to the next to facilitate a smooth learning process.

Remember that effective teaching involves guiding your audience or students through concepts step-by-step. Define Specific, Measurable, Achievable, Realistic, and Timely (SMART) objectives for each lesson in your course outline.

Create the Content

With a well-structured outline in hand, it's time to create your course content. This content includes text, audio, video, images, and other digital materials. If you have professional experience in your course topic, you may have existing content that can be integrated into your course, saving you time and effort.

To develop your content, utilize the materials you gathered during the outline and research stages. Consider using written content, audio recordings, slides, or a combination of media types to engage your audience effectively. Enhance accessibility by adding titles, video captions, and, if applicable, background music.

Picking the Right Platform

To bring your course online, decide on the appropriate platform. If you already have a professional website, you can integrate your online course as a dedicated section. Alternatively, create a new website solely for this purpose.

Several online teaching software options, such as Zoom, Google Meet, or Skype, facilitate virtual classes, live webinars, and online meetings. You can also explore platforms like eLearningX.org, Udemy, Coursera, or your website for hosting and distributing your course content.

If you're new to these tools, familiarize yourself with platforms like Zoom, webinars, Google Meet, podcasts, and YouTube to offer a variety of learning experiences.

Selling Your Course

You can then sell your online course. You can do this by allowing users to rent or purchase your online course video-by-video. When purchasing a video, users will enjoy unlimited streaming of the lesson they've purchased so they can review the content at all times. You can decide whether you want viewers to download or watch the video directly on your site.

You can also sell your course by letting the users subscribe to your channel for a monthly fee, setting up different payment options, offering the choice of paying in full or through a recurring payment plan, or having one-on-one real-time lessons, which will be paid as a fee. Alongside your paid lessons, be sure to also offer a small preview of your course entirely for free.

Getting a sneak peek of what they can expect to see will encourage students to sign up for the paid classes. Your free content can be in the form of a short trailer for each lesson, or you can offer the first lesson for free while the rest are paid.

Another idea for a freebee is to create a live Q&A session at the beginning of the course, inviting users to participate free of charge while generating interest. This will help you connect with fans in real-time. Whichever giveaway option you choose, the free version of your course will benefit in promoting your online course.

Pricing Your Course

You should also know how to price your online course. After filming your content, you might wonder how to price it. Here are some ways to determine your course fees.

First, do a quick audit to determine the average course price on your topic by checking on competitors' courses. While the prices can fluctuate depending on how much of an expert the course instructor is, try to get a sense of the going market rate for reference.

Consider how long it took you to create the course. Any business endeavor that aims to be profitable should have a good balance between time invested and profits gained. Also, factor in how your price gives good value to the user.

Marketing and Optimizing Your Course

After you've spent a lot of creative energy and valuable time creating your online course, it's time to promote it and get those course registrations through marketing your content. To market your online course, you can use free promotions and paid types of marketing.

You can even create a logo to help your course look professional and stand out as you promote it. You should take advantage of the digital opportunities to improve your curriculum by asking for feedback, such as during and after the course.

The more optimized and improved your course is, the more likely students will have a better experience, recommend you, or enroll in future workshops or learning opportunities you may offer. You can get feedback by creating surveys after every course or module.

Here, you can ask about students' experiences, suggestions for improvement, and anything else they hoped to get out of the course. Once you measure the success and analyze the answers, you can adjust and continue running better and better courses.

Cultivate a Community

Lastly, you can cultivate a learning community. Online education is mostly a solitary activity. Therefore, fostering a community of learners around your course will greatly improve their experience, contributing to the overall success of your course. An active online community can help users share their learning process with peers.

Together, they can celebrate their successes and raise any questions. In addition, students can bounce ideas off one another, generating a vibrant conversation and enhancing the interest and excitement around your class.

Your online community is also a good place to share news about upcoming courses or other opportunities that might interest this already engaged audience.

Three Essential Factors to Consider

Before embarking on creating and teaching an online course, three essential factors must be considered.

Factor 1: Know Your Target Audience

First and foremost, knowing your audience is paramount. Understanding their demographics, interests, and learning styles will allow you to effectively tailor the content to meet their needs, ensuring relevance and engagement.

Factor 2: Pick the Right Platform

The choice of platform is equally crucial. With numerous options available, such as Udemy, Coursera, eLearningX.org or hosting the course on your own website, selecting the right platform will enable you to reach your target audience and provide your students with a seamless, user-friendly experience.

Factor 3: Marketing it for Success

Determining the price of your online course requires careful consideration. Factor in the time and effort invested in creating it, the value it offers to students, and the pricing of similar courses in the market. Striking the right balance will ensure yours remains competitive and appealing.

Once the course is ready, a well-thought-out marketing strategy becomes essential to attract students and generate interest. Utilizing social media marketing, email campaigns, and content marketing will help in promoting the course effectively.

Additionally, several other elements contribute to the success of your online course. These include the format of the course, its length, mode of delivery, assessment methods, level of support provided, and the type of certificate offered.

By carefully considering and aligning all these factors with your target audience and learning objectives, you can create a comprehensive and effective online course that impacts your student's learning journey.

Summary

Creating an online course can be a great way to meet the growing demand for education and generate revenue. However, before creating an online course, it is essential to understand the steps involved in the process.

This includes choosing the right subject matter, testing your idea, researching the topic extensively, creating a course outline, developing the course content, bringing the course online, marketing the content, gathering feedback, and building a learning community. By imparting knowledge and expertise through an online course, you can establish yourself as an authority in your field, foster a community of like-minded individuals, and expand your reach – all from the comfort of your home.

Choosing a subject that appeals to both you and your students and that you are passionate about is important. You should also research the demand for the topic and gather feedback from your audience to ensure the success of your course.

• **Identify your target audience:** Understand who your course is for and their needs and pain points. This will help you create content that is relevant and valuable to them.

• **Define your course objectives**: Clearly define what you want your students to learn and be able to do by the end of the course.

• **Choose a format:** Decide on the format of your course, whether it's a series of video lectures, a self-paced e-book, or a combination of both.

- **Develop a course outline:** Create an outline of your course content, including the topics you will cover, the order in which you will cover them, and any assessments or quizzes you will include.

- **Create high-quality content:** Invest time and effort in creating engaging and informative content that is easy to understand and follow.

- **Test and refine:** Before launching your course, test it with a small group of beta testers and make any necessary adjustments based on their feedback.

- **Promotion plan:** Create a promotion plan for your course, including social media, email marketing, and paid advertising.

- **Consider monetizing:** Decide whether or not you want to monetize your course, and choose the pricing model that best suits your goals.

- **Be prepared for ongoing maintenance:** Keep in mind that creating an online course is an ongoing process, and you'll need to continue to update and maintain it over time.

- **Be passionate:** Be passionate about the subject matter and willing to put in the time and effort to create a high-quality course to help your students achieve their goals.

Chapter 6: Picking Your Niche

The first crucial step is selecting your niche when embarking on a business venture, such as teaching online courses. Having a well-defined niche offers several advantages, including audience growth, opportunities for sponsorships and partnerships, and the ability to focus your marketing and content creation efforts effectively.

Benefits of Selecting a Niche

A niche represents the specific area of expertise you choose to specialize in. It guides the products you develop, the partnerships you pursue, the content you create, and the customers you aim to attract.

With thousands and thousands of niches, you should find one specific market you can serve rather than spreading yourself too thin by trying to operate in multiple niche markets.

Enhanced Profitability

Not all niches are profitable for online business, and not all will appeal to you. The most successful online businesses combine the entrepreneur's interest with a popular and searchable topic that people are willing to spend money on to learn about or add to their lives. Everything about marketing comes down to the audience – your target audience.

When your business has a clearly defined niche, you can attract even more business from your ideal customers and often command higher fees.

Make Easier Decisions

Each business has a unique audience. Once you identify your audience, every marketing decision you make becomes easier because you can gather data to help you find that student, and you can begin building your service offerings and marketing campaigns around their needs.

Leverage Your Strengths

It's essential to acknowledge that you can't be an expert in every field (unless you employ a large team of specialists). Moreover, presenting a portfolio of diverse work can appear unfocused. By selectively choosing your niche, you can capitalize on your strengths and develop authority in that area.

Stand Out Against the Competition

Increase appeal with your niche audience because they will feel confident working with an authority who understands their needs. Referral partners will be easier to find because you can work with those who also work within your niche, plus those who focus on a complementary niche.

More importantly, the narrower your focus, the better your chance of standing out. You can become the go-to choose for clients/students who need what you have to offer. You may be able to raise your rates due to your specialty area of focus.

Improved Client Trust and Authority

When you specialize in a particular niche, it fosters trust and authority within your target audience. Clients are more likely to trust your expertise when they perceive you as an authority in your chosen field. This trust translates into stronger client relationships, often leading to repeat business and referrals.

Focused Content Creation

A well-defined niche allows you to create content that resonates deeply with your audience. You can tailor your blog posts, videos, webinars, and other content to address your niche audience's specific pain points and interests. This focused content is more likely to attract and engage your target demographic.

Streamlined Marketing Efforts

Marketing becomes more efficient and cost-effective when you concentrate on a niche. You can direct your advertising and promotional efforts toward platforms and channels where your niche audience is most active, ensuring that your message reaches the right people.

Sustainability and Longevity

Specializing in a niche can contribute to the long-term sustainability of your business. A well-defined niche often has a more stable and loyal customer base, reducing the impact of market fluctuations. It can also lead to product and service expansion opportunities within your niche.

Market Research Advantage

By focusing on a niche, you can deeply understand your target audience's preferences, behaviors, and pain points. This knowledge is invaluable for creating products and services that precisely meet your audience's needs, giving you a competitive edge.

How to Find Your Niche

Research your niche before you settle on it – it's important to investigate the demand within that niche, the opportunities and risks, plus the competitive landscape.

The following are several ways you can research a potential niche.

Conduct Surveys and Interviews

One of the best ways to understand a market is to go right to the source. You can do this by conducting surveys, interviews, or focus groups with your intended audience. Ask important questions about what influences their buying decisions, how much they spend on related services annually, what they like and dislike about competitor solutions, what issues they need solving, and how you can meet their needs.

You may also want to purchase a mailing list or find other ways to reach your intended audience.

Look for Industry Data

Use Google to research your target industry or demographic through trade associations and related firms that survey market demand. These organizations can help determine if your niche is growing and how much demand there is for related products and services.

In addition, check your local library for a copy of the Encyclopaedia of Associations. If you have trouble finding what you need online, ask staff at your local library for help. There are all kinds of reference books and databases available free of charge.

Investigate Search Demand

Internet search data allows you to understand the demand for a keyword or phrase. You can interpret this information one of two ways. First, an extremely popular search term demonstrates there is market demand. The downside of this information is that the competitive landscape will likely be greater online because other website owners are also using this data.

A search term with slightly less popularity can still show you there is market demand but may also be easier to penetrate as the competition will likely be smaller.

Evaluate the Competition

Understanding your competition is essential to determining whether your business can find a competitive edge in a new market. This helps position your strengths against their weaknesses while also allowing you to prepare answers when asked about potential advantages the competitors had. You can use the internet to find a myriad of information.

Start with your top five to ten competitors. Check what products and services they offer, how much they charge, and what advantages they might have against you. You can also sign up for their mailing lists or ask for additional details. Don't be shy about this kind of research. You can bet they will be watching you, too.

Making the Decision to Shift Your Focus

As you transition to focus on a specific niche, know that you don't have to turn away from other businesses completely. If you're worried that narrowing your focus could create a cash crunch, then gradually make the change. Begin to focus your marketing efforts on reaching your newly defined audience while you continue to accept other work.

Over time, your marketing should catch up, and you will discover how much easier it is to generate business when your target audience is clearly defined and your services align with their needs. You might even reach a point where you are too busy with your niche work to accept other jobs – if so, you will need to hire some additional help.

Growing pains like this can be a good problem, but don't let high demand harm your ability to deliver great service or accept new clients. I've seen too many service providers turn away business because they couldn't keep up with demand, which makes no sense to me!

Do your best to stay one step ahead of the growth. Eventually, you may want to develop strategic relationships with companies that provide the services you no longer offer. Ideally, you will ally to refer business to each other continuously.

Develop Your Niche Identity

Once you have identified your niche focus, everything you do must convey that to your new audience. That means changing marketing materials, website content, advertising, and sales scripts. Some companies will need to change their entire brand identity as a result (for those who never really had one, to begin with, this will be a powerful exercise in improving focus). Assemble a new portfolio for your website and sales calls, along with marketing collateral that explains your services' benefits, photos, and testimonials.

Identifying Your Unique Difference

Within your niche, there will undoubtedly be competitors in your field (if there aren't, then your niche might be too narrowly defined). To really stand out and **Own Your Niche**, you need to understand what sets you apart from the rest. You could consider yourself to be the best in your field, but you need to know how you will convey that to prospective customers.

What makes your business different from your competitors?

The ability to answer this question powerfully can put you on the right track to **Own Your Niche**.

Consider Reputation

People are likelier to tell ten friends about a bad experience than a good one. To get clients talking about your services and recommending them to peers and friends, their experience has to be extraordinary. Reputation can make or break a business. The business can also cultivate a reputation. Remember, reputation matters. While developing the new brand positioning for your business, consider the reputation and what you want your company to be known for.

Avoid anything highlighting your weaknesses – and know that all companies have weaknesses. Focus on drawing out the best in your company.

Positioning Questions:
- Do you currently offer services that generate rave reviews? If not, how could you improve your customer experience?

- What is unique about your business versus the competition?

- What do you want your business to be known for?

- What values do you hold in high importance?

- Could your values or belief system become part of your brand positioning?

In the marketing world, every marketing firm has what is known as a 'swipe file.' This is where ideas from other businesses are kept, which can include postcards with interesting offers, attention-grabbing sales letters, or smart print advertisements. The point of a swipe file is never to steal ideas but to learn from others and use the materials for inspiration.

When you transfer this concept to your business, you can benefit in many ways. You can spark new ideas by studying your competitors and companies outside of your industry. Take that a step further; you can even ask your competitors for ideas.

Sounds crazy?

Keep reading.

How could you reach out to others who do what you do?

What questions would you ask if you had the chance?

Why not take that chance and ask?

Study companies in your industry that are successful. You don't have to contact competitors to learn from them. You can also sit back and study what they're doing. You can learn a lot simply from visiting websites or reading marketing collateral. Study their services, how they position themselves, and what you like and don't like about how they're doing business.

Also, pay attention to where they advertise and what media coverage they've received.

When it comes to competitors, don't waste energy worrying about them, but try to keep your finger on the pulse of what's going on. It's important to understand their strengths and weaknesses and how they compare with yours so that you are prepared to respond to questions about how your company differs when you're on a sales call with a prospective client.

You can also draw inspiration from businesses outside of your industry. For example, loyalty programs work well with many retail businesses.

How could you use something like that in your business?

Become a student of life, pay attention to how other companies operate, and then figure out how to apply those lessons to your business.

Choosing a niche for your business makes building a business easier and faster by:

- Allowing you to concentrate your efforts on a single area of expertise.

- Connecting you with a focused and interested audience.

- Making your business more searchable online.

- Helping you connect with advertisers, sponsors, or other businesses.

- Giving your business a clear direction for developing content or choosing products to sell.

- Simplifying your marketing by giving you a clear message about purpose and benefits.

Summary

To begin choosing the right niche for your online business, start by brainstorming a list of potential niches. Consider interests you actively participate in, hobbies you'd be willing to turn into a business, any specialties or training you possess, and previous work experiences that could be transformed into a business venture. Once you have a list, narrow it down to the top five ideas that genuinely interest you and align with your passion. Remember that committing to a business requires time and dedication, so choosing a niche you are passionate about will fuel your motivation to work hard and make it a success.

After shortlisting your ideas, it's time to research them thoroughly to determine which one has the most potential to become a profitable online business. Here are some steps you can take:

1. Conduct a Google search to gauge the popularity potential of each niche. Look for many search results, including dedicated websites, articles, blogs, products, and other online businesses in the niche. Competition is a positive sign, indicating a

market with interested customers. If you find limited results, there may not be sufficient online demand for that niche.

2. Utilize keyword resources like Google Ads, Keyword Planner, or Answer the Public to search for related keywords. Look for popular search terms that many people are actively searching for. Discovering over 10,000 searches per month for the main keyword and 50,000 searches for related but more specific keywords indicates a strong niche with potential.

3. Check offline sources by visiting local bookstores or magazine stands. If you find publications covering your niche, it suggests profit potential in that market. Also, look for digital publications related to the niche for further research and potential opportunities to establish your expertise and market your business.

4. Search affiliate marketing sites like Clickbank for products related to your potential niche. A wide range of available products indicates a ready market for your chosen niche.

5. Examine social media platforms like Instagram to identify popular hashtags and content related to your niche. The number of followers and users of such content will give you an idea of the niche's audience size.

Explore broad topics and more specific aspects of each niche during your research. For example, if your niche is yoga, delve into areas like yoga videos, yoga gear, yoga courses, or yoga for beginners. This will help you narrow down your niche and determine your specialty.

Upon completing your research, you should clearly understand which niche holds the most profit potential for your online business. Additionally, you will gain insights into potential products to sell, the target audience interested in your niche, suitable keywords for search engine optimization, and ideas for growing your social media presence. Armed with this information and a well-defined niche, you can confidently launch and grow your online business, ensuring a quicker, smoother, and more profitable journey.

Chapter 7: How to Structure and Outline Your Online Course

A course outline defines the fundamental components required to be taught by all instructors, while a syllabus details how an individual instructor will teach the course, encompassing specific assignments, dates, grading standards, and other conduct rules required by that instructor.

A syllabus may encompass methods and topics that exceed the course outline, with the understanding that all content in the course outline must be taught by all instructor. The objective is to develop an integrated course outline, where the course content, instructional methods, evaluation, and assignments coalesce, aligning with the achievement of the course's learning outcomes.

An effective course outline contains critical details: course name and description, schedule, learning outcomes, learning/assessment tasks, assessments submission procedures, due dates, assessment criteria, prescribed and recommended readings, assessment grades, and student responsibilities.

Creating an online course involves serval steps. Understanding the overall process before outlining your course is crucial as it distinguish between a course that sells successfully and one that flops.

So, what's the key to crafting a successful course?

The Art of Crafting Online Courses - Problem Solving to Perfect Packaging
Solve A Problem

First, there is your course topic. It needs to do one thing: solve a problem that people care so much about that they're willing to pay for it. For instance, some people wouldn't pay to learn how to bake sourdough bread. But other people care about their lack of sourdough baking skills and are willing to pay for a course that teaches them how to do it.

Ask yourself:

- What problem does your course solve?

- Is there a paying audience for that topic?

When you know what problem, your course helps solve, you can create a course outline focusing on that one thing.

Define Your Target Audience

Next, understand *who* your ideal clients/students are. Identifying your course audience is crucial for your outline. After all, your course teaching style will change depending on your audience.

Will your learners be adults, kids, teens, college students, corporate professionals, or small business owners?

And you need to know how to talk to them about your course. If you use jargon or technical terms or go into technical details too soon, you might confuse your audience, depending on who they are.

Create Your Course Material

While you need a course outline to sell your course (to know WHAT you're selling), you shouldn't create your course material just yet. You must start with the smallest course possible to successfully sell your first course.

Too many aspiring course creators try to turn their first course into a complete flagship course with all the bells and whistles, which is way too overwhelming to create and sell. Instead, focus on a 'First Steps' course that makes it much easier to create, sell and over-deliver on it.

A First Steps course teaches the first steps people need to take to achieve their ultimate goal.

What's more, you don't create your course right away. Instead, please start with the outline and the first module or units before you sell it. Once you've sold it to your first students, you create the rest of your course in real-time based on student feedback. This way, you create the *best* course on your topic based on what students actually want.

So, to be super clear, you'll create a rough outline so that you know *what* you teach in your course and then add or remove things as you teach your course. Now, if you feel you absolutely want to create your course before selling it, you can. But make sure you're not just doing it because you think that will be the higher value or more perfect.

Most course creators have experience with the subject they're teaching but not so much experience teaching it. When you create your course based on live feedback, you can create the best value and experience for your clients.

Package and Price Your Course

The next step is to package and price your course. Packaging your course means getting clear on how you will sell it as a standalone product.

- What's the transformation people get when they implement it?

- What is included in your course?

- What bonuses do you offer?

- Do you offer coaching calls or other support?

- And what does your pricing look like?

If you're creating a First Steps course, it'll be less comprehensive than a flagship course, so you'd price it accordingly.

Outlining Your Online Course

A course outline helps you create your course faster and better. It offers a map of your course for yourself and your students. Here's how to create an outline, from creating a template to filling it in with a clear structure. Your outline isn't necessarily the final one you'll use because you might modify it based on student feedback. But it still gives the overall picture of what your course will teach and its outcomes.

Step 1: Create An Online Course Outline Template

The first step is to create the bare bones of your course outline. Next, you'll include more details.

Define Your Learning Outcomes

First, get clear on your course's learning outcomes. The transformation you offer is the most important part of your course, so don't skip this step. However, this part doesn't have to be very long; a few sentences are enough.

What Should Be Included in A Course Outline?

Your course outline should include:

- **Course Name**

- **Course Description:** Describe your course and what the end goal people get when they go through it.

- **Course Schedule:** This outlines when you'll create each step of the course.

- **Modules**

- **Lessons:** Add the lessons you'll include under each module.

- **Bonuses:** Include an overview of the bonuses you'll include.

After creating a course outline template, you should know how to implement it.

Step 2: Structure Your Online Course

Using your outline template, you should proceed as follows. That way, you'll structure a course that helps your students get the best results.

Identify the Main Milestones: The first step to creating your perfect outline is to identify the main milestones your students will pass through while following your course. These milestones support the overall goal they're working towards. If your course requires students to achieve certain goals before moving on to the next module, you will organize your outline according to those goals.

The second way to organize your content is through distinct areas of mastery. These milestones might not necessarily be part of a linear process, but they are distinct areas or benchmarks your student must master before reaching the final destination. Organizing your course lets you know what to include in each module.

Name Your Course and Describe It: Before you create your modules, you need a course name. Think about words related to your course. You don't want to be too creative here; instead, use a clear name. Also, include a brief description. You can use the learning outcomes you brainstormed in the previous step as your course description.

Plan your Modules and Lessons: The next step is to plan your modules and lessons. Your course needs to be easy to follow so that your students achieve their learning outcomes.

A common mistake many first-time course creators make is to include as much as they can in their course because they mistake information for value. But your students don't care about how many lessons you include or how many PDFs they get; they care about results.

And that's why the best courses include *only* the information people need to implement it and get results. Your course should include 4–8 modules to be easy to implement. Each module should have no more than 3–7 lessons. Fill in the course outline template with your modules based on the milestones you defined earlier in this section.

When creating your lessons, focus on:

- Creating an introduction in each lesson where you tell students what they'll learn in that lesson

- Sharing results-focused content, not just information

- Summarising the main takeaways and letting your students know what they should do next at the end of each lesson

You also need to specify how you'll deliver the content.

Are you using audio, video, or text?

Or a combination of all three?

And what supporting material are you including in your modules?

Make sure to include a list of that material (notes, checklists, implementation guides, trackers, etc.).

- **Decide on Your Course Bonuses:** Finally, you need to include bonuses, so your course offer feels like a no-brainer for your students. Your bonuses depend on your course, but a few examples include:

1. Results trackers

2. Templates

3. Scripts

4. Case studies

5. Bonus lessons

Include a list of your bonuses in your outline. And that's it. You're done with your outline!

Step 3: Apply Critical Thinking

The incorporation of critical thinking must be evident throughout the course outline, especially in the course content, instructional methods, representative assignments, and evaluation methods. It must be clear that students are expected to think critically, instructed in how to do so (instructional methods), asked to practice critical thinking in outside assignments (representative assignments), and are held accountable for their performance (methods of evaluation).

As a teacher, you should create a topical outline containing a complete list of all topics to be taught in the course. The outline should be arranged by topics with sub-topics (i.e., major and minor headings). Content may be typed directly into the screen using the outline tools or the 'Paste from Word' icon.

A good course outline should elicit a list of possible methods that could be used to teach the course. Remember that you're indicating the instructional methods that will lead students to achieve the course learning outcomes. For degree-applicable and transferrable courses, methods of instruction must elicit college-level effort and effectively teach critical thinking.

The course outline has several advantages for the implementing institute or, in this case, you as an instructor. First, it provides a very flexible and rich platform for almost all components of online courses. Second, it provides a common template for you or other instructors, which is valuable if instructors enhance or update other courses created by others in past semesters. Third, it becomes easier for a student to navigate several courses if the template and structure are the same. Fourth, grouping relevant items in the same place and categorizing them according to learner expectations should enhance the efficiency of the online courses.

Creating a course outline helps you organize your ideas. Putting an outline together first allows you to create a much more effective course. There may be many topics you want to cover. An outline allows you to organize these topics in a way that makes sense to your students. In addition, it prevents you from forgetting to add critical information that is relevant to the topic.

Writing out what you plan to cover will also help you generate ideas. One idea leads to another, which leads to another, providing you with deeper and more information-rich content.

Three Crucial Steps to Remember

Consider these three critical steps before developing the curriculum for an online course:

1.   **Define the End Objective:** Identifying the end goal of your course is the first essential step in creating an effective curriculum. Your end goal should be specific, measurable, and aligned with the needs and interests of your target audience. It should also be achievable by the end of the course.

2.   **Bridge the Gap:** Once you have identified the end goal, you must determine the knowledge and skills your students need to acquire to acquire to achieve that goal. This may involve identifying gaps in their current understanding and determining what content must be covered to bridge those gaps.

3.   **Choose the Best Mediums:** After determining the content that needs to be covered, select the best mediums for delivering that content. These can include text, audio, video, images, and interactive activities. The chosen mediums should align with the learning styles and preferences of your target audience and the end goal of your course.

Following these steps will provide you with a clear structure and outline for your online course, helping you create a comprehensive and effective curriculum that aligns with your target audience and learning objectives. It's also important to mention that testing the course, getting feedback, and making adjustments are crucial steps in curriculum development.

Summary

Primarily, structuring and outlining an online course involves creating a plan or roadmap for the content covered in the course.

It is paramount to first consider the goals and objectives of the course. These should be specific, measurable, and aligned with the overall curriculum or program. Once these are established, the course can be broken down into smaller, more manageable sections or modules. Each module should have a specific theme or topic and include various types of content such as readings, videos, quizzes, and discussions.

When outlining the course, it is important to consider the logical flow and progression of the material. The course should be organized to build on previous knowledge and gradually introduce new concepts. This can be achieved using a thematic or chronological approach or grouping similar concepts.

It is also important to consider the appropriate assessment methods for the course. This can include quizzes, exams, written assignments, and participation in online discussions. The assessment methods should align with the course goals and objectives and provide a clear understanding of student progress and understanding.

It's also essential to consider the course design and layout. The course should be visually pleasing and easy to navigate, with clear instructions and navigation buttons. It should be accessible to all students, including those with disabilities.

Online courses should also include interaction and engagement with the students; this can be done through different activities, such as discussion boards, group projects, and peer evaluations, which help keep students engaged and motivated.

These are the key guidelines when thinking of creating an online course:

1. Solve a problem

2. Define your target audience

3. Create your course material

4. Package and price your course

Chapter 8: Curriculum Development

Curriculum design is a purposeful and conscious planning effort to improve student learning. It involves identifying clear objectives and utilizing a systematic process to create effective educational experiences. The design must be creative, allowing for innovative thinking and adaptation at various stages. While perfection is not the goal, compromises are made to develop a curriculum that works well within its constraints.

To design a great course curriculum, one should consider educational purposes, organize instruction around active learning, foster language competence, emphasize learning techniques, and offer individualized learning paths. A work-study approach and inquiry-based learning can also enhance the curriculum. An environmental focus can integrate physical, biological, and social issues into all subjects.

Strategic planning involves setting goals, determining actions, and mapping them over time using available resources. Understanding the learners' needs and interests is crucial, and feedback from potential students can aid in designing the curriculum.

Course objectives should be specific, measurable, attainable, relevant, and time-bound. Collaboration among instructors, evidence-based analysis, student-focused enhancement, and continuous improvement should guide the curriculum design process.

Content should align with learning outcomes, reflect real-world applications, and be pitched appropriately. The learning program and timetable should logically sequence learning elements to enable student progression. The choice of teaching and learning methods is essential, focusing on placing propositional knowledge into real-world contexts. Proper consideration of resources is essential for successful curriculum implementation.

Once the curriculum has been fully developed, it is ready for implementation. Those involved with implementation (usually teachers and examiners as well as students) need to interpret the curriculum in the same way as it is put into practice.

The course is broken into modules at the beginning of the design process, immediately allocating these to relevant course team members. Module design often takes place in isolation from the wider course until the modules are brought back together before approval. Although this may offer a swift distribution of the design workload, it does not provide the best environment for constructive alignment of course/course aims, the learning, teaching, and assessment strategy, and the strengths of the course team, which can create a diffuse and disjointed course identity and offering. Pre-testing or piloting can help to identify problems and issues and how a course works in practice.

Preparing an effective course or curriculum provides an educator with a unique opportunity to consider, at the same time, the needs of learners and teachers/instructors and the interaction among them. A good curriculum recognizes learning as an active, constructive, contextual process.

It will provide guidance that helps educators enable learners to acquire new knowledge and skills and apply them in various contexts. The careful alignment of aims, learning outcomes, teaching approaches, and assessment methods inherent in excellent curriculum design places educators in the best possible position to create an environment that supports student learning.

As a teacher/instructor, you should align the course objectives in your modules and lessons. Also, chunk your lessons into bits to avoid overwhelming your students with information. Curriculum-design processes are essential to effective learning experiences across education and professional contexts.

Without effective curriculum-design processes, learners often lack the structure and guidance necessary for optimal learning, and organizations cannot effectively measure results and optimize their return on investments. While we have all experienced curricula, curriculum design is changing, becoming more complex, and incorporating new technologies and strategies.

One of the most profound shifts is expanding the scope of curriculum design to consider how the curriculum connects to broader and more networked learning environments. Curriculum design is an essential skill for emerging education and learning professionals and will continue to be a dynamic, innovative, and exciting field of practice for years to come.

As learning design and technology innovations are created and scaled, curriculum-design processes must adapt to ensure these methods remain grounded in effective learning practices. This section discusses several innovation trends and their possible implications on curriculum-design processes.

The Three Popular Ways to Design a Curriculum

One of the foundational innovations influencing curriculum-design processes is a shift from individual-focused to team-based curriculum design. Curriculum design is becoming more of a team support where people from diverse backgrounds, professions, and areas of expertise work together to create a curriculum.

The three most popular ways of developing a course curriculum are as follows.

1.   **Need-based Curriculum:** This is developed based on the specific needs and goals of the target audience and is often used in professional development and training programs. It addresses the immediate needs of the learners and is designed to help them acquire the skills and knowledge they need to perform their jobs or meet specific goals.

2.   **Academic-based Curriculum:** This is developed based on the standards and guidelines of a specific academic field or discipline. It is often used in higher education and is designed to help students acquire the knowledge and skills they need to succeed in a particular field of study.

3.   **Experience-based/expert-based Curriculum:** This is developed based on the instructor's or subject matter expert's real-world experience and expertise. It is often used in professional development and training programs and is designed to help learners acquire the skills and knowledge they need to excel in their field.

Each of these ways has its advantages and disadvantages, and the choice of one depends on the type of course and the target student. But you should know the following:

- A need-based curriculum can be highly practical and focused on real-world applications.

- An academic-based curriculum can offer a solid foundation in a particular field.

- An experience-based curriculum can offer a unique perspective and valuable insights.

When choosing a specific approach, it's important to consider the course's learning objectives and the target audience's needs and goals.

Need-Based Curriculum

Many decisions that impact a course's success occur well before the first day of class. Thoughtful planning during the curriculum design phase makes teaching more manageable and enjoyable and enhances student learning. Once your course is meticulously planned, the teaching process involves daily implementation of your course design.

To design an effective need-based curriculum course, you should:

Consider Timing and Logistics

The precise timing depends on whether the course is new or has been offered before, how much time you have to prepare departmental differences and individual preferences. While this timeline is not exhaustive or applicable to every course, it serves as a general guide for standard courses.

Recognize Who Your Students Are

Students are not only intellectual but also social and emotional beings, and all these dimensions interact to impact learning and performance. When planning an effective course, it is crucial to consider who your students are by taking into account their prior knowledge.

According to Bransford, Brown, and Cocking in "How People Learn" (2000, p. 10), students enter formal education with prior knowledge, skills, beliefs, and concepts that significantly shape what they observe in their environment and how they organize and interpret it.

This, in turn, affects their ability to recall, reason, solve problems, and acquire new knowledge. New knowledge builds upon existing knowledge. Therefore, assessing what your students are likely to know before entering your course and how well they know it is vital when designing a curriculum.

If your course is part of a sequence of courses, it is beneficial to ascertain what material has been covered in the course preceding it. You can do this by talking to a colleague who has taught the preceding course or asking for a copy of their syllabus, assignments, and/or exams.

Consider not only what topics have been covered but the extent to which students have been asked to apply particular skills and knowledge.

For example, are they required simply to identify theories or do something more sophisticated, such as make predictions based on different theoretical orientations?

Are they simply required to analyze aspects of stagecraft and lighting, or have they used these insights to create their own designs?

The extent to which students have been required to actively do something with what they have learned will determine how deeply they know it.

Teaching Based on Skills

It is also advisable to communicate with colleagues teaching downstream courses, i.e., courses that follow yours in the sequence. This communication can help you discern the skills and knowledge expected of students as they exit your course. This understanding will aid in determining the appropriate scope and pace of your course.

Another useful practice during course planning is to examine your students' majors listed on the course roster or, in their absence, consult a departmental colleague for insights into the likely composition of your student body. If the majority of your students come from within your discipline, it may be reasonable to assume they possess certain background knowledge, skills, and experience. Conversely, if a significant number of students hail from outside your discipline, you may need to adjust your approach.

Checking students' majors in advance can also guide you in leveraging their prior knowledge to make course material relevant and engaging. For instance, if several students in an anthropology class have backgrounds in design, incorporating examples and illustrations related to diverse cultural aesthetics or the use of objects in various cultural contexts can help students connect their disciplinary knowledge to new material and understand its relevance to their interests and future endeavors.

Assess Their Knowledge

New knowledge cannot be built effectively on a weak foundation; thus, it is important to determine where students' prior knowledge is fragile, where it contains inaccuracies, naive assumptions, and misunderstandings of the contexts and conditions in which to apply particular skills.

There are several ways to assess students' prior knowledge. One easy way is to administer a simple diagnostic pre-test during the first week of class. A well-designed pre-test can identify areas of robust or weak understanding.

If mastery of prerequisite skills is poor across most students, you may have to adjust the pace or scope of the course accordingly. Suppose a small number of individuals lack the necessary skills. In that case, this information can help you advise them appropriately, perhaps to seek outside tutoring or even, in some cases, to drop the class.

Another way to assess students' prior knowledge early in the semester is to ask them to draw a concept map illustrating a key topic from your course. A glance at the concept maps students draw can give you a good sense of how well students currently understand the issue and help you identify misconceptions and inaccuracies.

Identify The Situational Constraints

To effectively plan your course, you should consider several factors, including:

- How big is your class?

- How many hours is each session?

- How many units are attached?

- What time of day is the class scheduled for?

- How long and frequent are the class meetings?

- Is this course required or elective?

- How many class meetings do you have over a semester?

- To what extent are you in control of the course and syllabus design process?

- What curricular goals does the institution or department have that affect this course or program?

- What technology are you using or is available?

- What software will you need?

- As a teacher, you should not assume anything. If you teach in a professional program, do your students have other commitments, such as full-time jobs?

These factors will determine how students can engage in the course. Additionally, consider students' time and flexibility to meet course requirements, their motivations for enrolling, and their prior experiences to create an inclusive learning environment.

Articulate and Align Your Learning Objectives

Before deciding on course content, establish a robust internal structure that fosters student learning. Alignment among objectives, assessments, and instructional strategies ensures a consistent structure within the course.

Alignment among objectives, assessments, and instructional strategies ensures an internally consistent structure. Alignment is when the objectives articulate the knowledge and skills you want students to acquire by the end of the course, and assessments allow the instructor to check the degree to which the students are meeting the learning objectives and instructional strategies are chosen to foster student learning towards meeting the objectives.

When these components are not aligned, students might rightfully complain that the test did not relate to what was covered in class, or instructors might feel that even though students are earning a passing grade, they haven't mastered the material at the desired level.

One way to approach course design is to start from the learning objectives, then move on to the other two components, and revisit the cycle iteratively as needed.

Articulating your learning objectives will help you select and organize course content, determine appropriate assessments and instructional strategies, and help the students direct their learning efforts appropriately and monitor their progress.

Student-Centered Learning Objectives

Learning objectives should be student-centered. Instructors often have a good idea of what they want to accomplish in a given course; they might want to cover certain topics or teach students certain ideas and skills.

You should also think in terms of what you want the students to be able to do at the end of the course. It is very helpful to articulate learning objectives by completing this prompt:

"At the end of the course, students should be able to _____."

Learning objectives should break down the task and focus on specific cognitive processes.

Many activities that faculty believe require a single skill involve synthesizing many component skills. To master these complex skills, students must practice and gain proficiency in the discrete component skills. For example, writing may involve identifying an argument, enlisting appropriate evidence, and organizing paragraphs, and problem-solving may require defining the problem's parameters, choosing appropriate formulas, etc.

Breaking down the skills will allow one to select appropriate assessments and instructional strategies so that students practice all component skills.

The Significance of Action Verbs

Learning objectives should use action verbs. Using action verbs lets you more easily measure the degree to which students can do what you expect them to do. Focusing on concrete actions and behaviors allows teachers to make student learning explicit and communicates to students the kind of intellectual effort we expect of them.

Measurable Learning Objectives

Learning objectives should be measurable in that they point to a clear assessment that can easily check whether students have mastered that skill; they should guide the selection of assessments and not be vague.

Identify Potential Assessments

Assessments should provide the instructors and the students with evidence of how well they have learned and what teachers intend them to learn. What instructors/teachers want students to learn and be able to do should guide the choice and design of the assessment.

Aligning Assessments

There are two major reasons for aligning assessments with learning objectives. First, alignment increases the probability that we will provide students with the opportunities to acquire and practice the knowledge and skills required on the various assessments on teachers' design.

Second, when assessments and objectives are aligned, good grades/performance are more likely to translate into good learning. When objectives and assessments are misaligned, many students will focus on activities that will lead to good grades on assessments rather than focusing on learning what teachers believe is important.

Assessment Activities

Many different types of activities can be used to assess students' proficiency in a given learning objective, and the same activity can be used to assess different objectives. To ensure a more accurate assessment of student proficiencies, it is recommended that teachers use different kinds of activities so that students have multiple ways to practice and demonstrate their knowledge and skills.

When deciding what kind of assessment activities to use, it is helpful to remember the following questions.

- What will the students' work on the activity tell me about their level of competence on the targeted learning objectives?

- How will the instructor's assessment of their work help guide students' practice and improve the quality of their work?

- And how will the assessment outcomes for the class guide the teacher's teaching practice?

Instructional Strategies

You can also identify appropriate instructional strategies. After selecting the learning objectives and assessments for the course, teachers must consider the various instructional activities they will use to engage students with the material and enable them to meet the objectives.

Of course, aligning instructional strategies with the other two components is key. Many instructional strategies are flexible and can be used to serve several learning objectives, but some are better suited for a particular set of objectives. In most cases, you must use a combination of instructional strategies.

For example, lectures can transmit information that:

- Supplements or enhanced reading

- Promote understanding via explanations

- Respond to student misconceptions or difficulties

- Create or engage interest in a new area

- And motivate reading or other assignments.

Discussions can help students:

- Practice thinking and communicating in the subject/discipline

- Evaluate positions, arguments, or designs

- Defend their own position

- Identify problems, conflicts, and inconsistencies

- Get feedback from/about students

- And draw on students' expertise and prior knowledge.

Case studies can actively involve students in learning to:

- Apply disciplinary methods of analysis

- Practice problem-solving

- Practice high-level cognitive skills

- Think critically

- Blend cognitive and affective dimensions

- Develop collaborative skills

- Relate knowledge to the real world

- And formulate arguments and counterarguments.

Writing can enable students to:

- Develop systematic relationships among ideas

- Application, analysis, synthesis, and evaluation

- Reflect on your own thinking

- Record the evolution of one's own thinking

- Practice disciplinary conventions

- And practice responding to feedback and revising

Group projects help students to:

- Compare and contrast perspectives

- Practice high-level cognitive skills

- Develop meta-skills such as leadership, communication, and conflict resolution

- And strategize and plan how to tackle complex problems and distribute work.

Other forms of instructional strategies can be recitations, public reviews, evaluations, service-learning, and independent student projects.

Summary

When designing an effective course, you should consider several key elements, including timing and logistics, students' needs and backgrounds, and connections to prior and future coursework.

First, the timing and logistics of the course must be considered. This includes determining the appropriate time needed for preparation, allowing for any departmental differences and individual preferences, and ensuring the class schedule and location are convenient for the students.

Next, it is important to recognize the unique needs and backgrounds of the students. Students are not just intellectual but also social and emotional beings, and all these dimensions interact to impact learning and performance.

Equally important is to connect the course to prior and future coursework. This includes determining what topics have been covered in previous courses and what skills and knowledge are expected in future courses. By understanding the connections between courses, the curriculum can be designed to build on previous knowledge and prepare students for future coursework.

Additionally, you should ensure the course material is relevant and engaging for the students. Understanding the students' majors and prior knowledge can tailor the material to their interests and needs. This can be done by using examples and illustrations that relate to their disciplinary knowledge and making connections to their future work.

Designing an effective course requires a thorough understanding of the student's needs, backgrounds, and connections to prior and future coursework. By considering these elements and incorporating them into the curriculum design, the course can be tailored to the student's needs, creating a strong foundation for new knowledge to be built on and allowing for effective student learning.

Academic-Based Curriculum

A crucial part of developing an effective, in-depth, and academic-based course curriculum involves improving students' learning, teaching, and assessment. Student learning increases when schools/colleges/universities or their teachers/instructors focus on understanding students' unique needs and capabilities.

Developing an effective, in-depth, academic-based course curriculum sets high expectations for every student and creates curriculum, instruction, and assessment that enable students to meet those expectations.

Developing such a course curriculum aims to communicate the best approach to curriculum development, teaching, and assessment. It offers specific tools that teachers and schools can use to design curricula, develop assessment tasks, and create classroom practices that will lead to significant student learning and growth.

Developing an effective, in-depth, and academic-based course curriculum helps schools/colleges/universities or teachers/instructors embrace the best principles, such as:

- Teaching a curriculum grounded in rigorous, public, academic standards, relevant to the concerns of adolescents, and based on how students learn best

- Using instructional methods designed to prepare all students to achieve high standards and become lifelong learners

- Creating staff middle-grade schools with teachers who are experts at teaching students and engaging teachers in ongoing professional development

- Organizing relationships for learning to create a climate of intellectual development and a caring community of shared educational purpose

- Governing democratically through direct or representative participation by all school/colleges/university staff members, the adults who know students best

- Providing safe and healthy schools/colleges/university environments as part of improving academic performance

- And developing caring and ethical citizens and involving parents and communities in supporting student learning and healthy development

These practices will translate into action in schools/colleges/universities and help teachers, institutions, leadership teams, and faculty committees engage in collaborative work.

An in-depth and academic-based curriculum will lead to the following:

Improve Learning, Teaching, and Assessment for All Students:

That is, working collaboratively to set high standards, close the achievement gap among students, develop curricula promoting mind and intellectual inquiry habits, utilize various instructional strategies and approaches, and emphasize literacy and numeracy teaching.

Building Leadership Capacity and a Professional Collaborative Culture

That is, creating a democratic school/college/university community, fostering skills and practices of strong leadership, establishing regular common planning time, and embedding professional development in the school/college/university's daily life.

Data-Based Inquiry and Decision Making

That is, setting a vision based on principles, collecting and analyzing multiple sources of data to help improve areas that most impact learning, teaching, and assessment, and setting annual measurable goals.

Creating a School Culture to Support High Achievement and Personal Development

That is, creating structures that promote a culture of high-quality learning and teaching, establishing small learning communities, eliminating tracking, lowering student-teacher ratios, and building parent and community partnerships.

Networking with Like-Minded Instructor's or Learning Institutions

Participating in network meetings and forums. Developing the capacity to support instructors/teachers/trainers or school/college/university change: building capacity through collaboration.

Meet the Needs

Developing a curriculum that meets the needs of students is a complex process that rarely follows a prescribed pattern and is crucial for any school or learning institution. Teachers may devise ideas for projects, themes, and activities on the way to work, in the middle of class, during a conversation with a colleague, and even in the shower.

Some teachers begin with a theme, while others start with habits of mind, they want their students to acquire. Some teachers use state frameworks and standards as a starting point for curriculum development; others build a unit from an idea for a project.

Identify the Purpose

Developing an effective, in-depth, and academic-based course curriculum is not to dictate how teachers should develop their curriculum but rather to propose certain basic principles. A great curriculum should respond to the unique educational and social needs of each or specific age group; it should be based on content standards, habits of mind, and thinking skills; and promote collaborative teaching, learning, and assessment opportunities that enable all students to achieve high standards.

In addition, it should encourage and call on teachers/instructors/trainers to develop curricula organized around themes and essential questions. Themes such as power, balance, relationships, and patterns are the big ideas that unify teaching and learning experiences. Essential questions are two to three important questions about a theme that students and teachers consider throughout a unit to provide focus and stimulate inquiry.

Focus on the Assessment Approach

Also, the approach to academic course development must integrate teaching and learning with ongoing assessment. Ongoing formal and informal assessments give teachers, administrators, and students an understanding of their progress and what they need to do to improve.

Raise the Level

One of the main goals of an effective, in-depth academic course design is to raise the level of discourse among teachers by helping them exchange ideas about student learning, instructional methods, and curriculum development. Using the best practices mentioned above to look at student and teacher work, teachers can engage in rigorous intellectual dialogue to help them reflect on their work.

Build a Community

Conversations with colleagues energize teachers and help them to learn from each other, often leading them to try new methods in the classroom. These conversations also draw teachers' attention to equity issues as they focus on the diverse instructional needs of all students.

Understanding of the Student

Effective, in-depth, academic-based course curricula should be grounded in an understanding of the student. Curriculum development and teaching methods should be based on understanding the student as an intellectually capable, complex person who is responsive to challenges.

In response to the unique needs of students, facilitators/teachers need to organize their instructional programs and adopt teaching and learning methods that are most effective within a certain age group of students. Therefore, effective, in-depth, and academic-based course curricula should recognize that students are capable of critical and complex thinking and develop these skills by using them.

They are also capable of responding with high achievement when challenged and engaged. They also show variability in themselves and need variety in their day and in what is asked of them. Furthermore, they need increasing autonomy, responsibility, and opportunities to demonstrate that they can behave responsibly and are willing to take risks if they believe they are in a safe and trusting environment.

Placing the needs and capabilities of students at the center of curriculum planning, teaching, and assessment makes student learning more active, engaging, and profound. This magnitude will only improve if teachers work collaboratively to create learning opportunities based on these beliefs.

Evaluate Performance

Teachers must gather evidence throughout a unit of study or period and, in a final, culminating project or performance. Early in the curriculum development process, teachers should focus on assessment and how students demonstrate that they have achieved the learning goals.

Instead of waiting until the end of a unit of study to create a test or assign a project, teachers create assessment activities at the beginning because the assessments help determine what students will be doing as the unit progresses. Teachers must devise various assessments, including projects, exhibitions, portfolios, and demonstrations, to accommodate their classrooms' wide range of learners.

Such assessments ask students to explain, interpret, apply, analyze, synthesize, solve problems, and communicate information. Teachers also should ask their students to demonstrate understanding of others and themselves as examples of how/what they have learned.

For example, teachers ask students to grapple with open-ended questions based on meaningful work to develop higher-order thinking skills and synthesize information to support their opinions with evidence.

Higher Standards

Believing that young adolescents are capable of high achievement means teachers must raise their expectations for the quality of student work and build in the support necessary to help all students meet higher standards. To allow students to demonstrate they can act responsibly, teachers must genuinely ask students to use good judgment by, for example, having them make public presentations and by giving them choices.

Giving students these opportunities may be a dramatic change for a school or any learning institution that focuses more on controlling students' behavior than letting them make decisions for themselves. Teachers should ensure that assessments are transparent, giving students a clear understanding of what is expected of them regarding the quality of their work and how it will be evaluated.

The Right Assessment Tools

Teachers can use rubrics, develop assessment criteria with students, and display models of exemplary work to help students understand what is expected of them. Rather than just giving students a grade that tells them how they did concern each other or to an unidentified standard, teachers can also use assessments that give students specific feedback to help them improve. Assessment tasks based on learning goals help students know what is important to learn and assist teachers in understanding how effective their teaching is.

Some characteristics of assessment are:

Transparent – students know the criteria, learning goals, and timing of assessment, drive curriculum planning and teaching; that is, what students are asked to do depends on how they will be asked to demonstrate their learning, takes many forms, including projects, exhibitions, portfolios, and demonstrations, helps students, teachers, and parents understand what a child knows and can do and allows them to understand what a child needs to do to improve ongoing, that is, it is tied to the learning goals and is used to inform curriculum planning, teaching, and professional development.

Also, it should be based on what facilitators/teachers want students to know and be able to do. All curriculum development, teaching, and assessment are tied to a broader definition of standards than the typical state standards, which tend to be content-focused.

Focus on Cognitive Skills

Effective, in-depth, academic-based course curricula include habits of mind, skills development, and in-depth study and go beyond state and local standards to define what students need to do to be thoughtful, caring, and valued members of the community. Students and teachers should be engaged in authentic, intellectual work.

All student work should have significance beyond the classroom. This work should be purposeful and rigorous and develop skills and knowledge that will prepare students for the future and beyond. Hence, the effective, in-depth, and academic-based course curriculum is often project-based.

Assessment should demonstrate that students can do important work. A crucial part of curriculum planning is developing formal and informal assessments to understand what students know and are learning concerning the learning goals. A coherent curriculum should be developed across the entire school or learning institution.

Three Major Goals

Good academic-based course curricula include three learning goals for students: habits of mind, skills, and content standards.

These goals should be kept at the forefront of the learning community for all to see and for students and staff to strive for. By focusing on more than just content standards, teachers/facilitators aim to teach students to become compassionate and caring individuals who can think critically, access and synthesize information, clearly communicate their ideas, and develop deep understanding.

A great, in-depth, academic-based course curriculum should encourage students and teachers to be engaged in authentic, intellectual work that has significance beyond the classroom. The learning institution or online platform has to determine what students should know and be able to drive curriculum development, teaching, and assessment.

This way, the focus will be on student learning and growth, not on how much material is covered in a year. It should also broaden the definition of standards to include how students use their minds, act, and interact with others.

Project Based Instruction

Project-based instruction provides increased opportunities for students to engage in authentic, intellectual work and creates a shift in the teacher's role. Sometimes, the teacher may be the facilitator who guides students in a discussion about their experiments, while at other times, the teacher may set up a project for students that includes gathering oral histories.

In another role, the teacher may model their writing to begin teaching students how to write a poem. Teachers will use teaching techniques that ask students to participate actively in learning and in applying knowledge, skills, and habits of mind.

For example, students would not only study outstanding published poetry but also write and publish their own poetry in magazines. In science, students will be expected to create their own hypotheses and test them through investigation and research.

A curriculum based on authentic, intellectual work is:

- Purposeful, rigorous, and related to the real world

- Focuses on developing complex and critical thinking skills

- Project-based and active, allowing students to use their energy and creativity to enhance their learning

- Balances depth and breadth of material

- Explores relationships and connections and integrates information across disciplines

- Based on a multiple-draft process where students receive feedback from teachers and others to improve their work

- Explicitly teaches literacy across all content areas

- Integrates themes, essential questions, and standards into the daily work of students

- Addresses the variety of student learning styles by using a wide range of methods

- Allows students and teachers to take on numerous roles and allows for reflection and self-assessment.

Summary

In summary, an effective, in-depth, academic-based course curriculum should comprise the following components:

Theme: This is the concept or big idea of the study. It should be an important concept to humanity and can be explored across disciplines, eras, and cultures.

For example, power, force, patterns, and freedom are all appropriate themes.

Essential Questions: This help focus students on the most important aspects of the theme. Teachers and students consider two or three substantive questions throughout the unit and examine them from multiple perspectives.

Learning Goals: These describe what students should learn and be able to do as a result of the unit of study and are divided into three areas: habits of mind, skills, and content standards.

Assessment: Divided into Ongoing Assessments, Culminating Assessments, and Reflection and Self-assessment, designed so that students and teachers know how they are progressing and what they must do to improve.

• **Ongoing Assessments** – The work and assignments show how students are doing as the unit progresses.

• **Culminating Assessments** – A project or performance that asks students to apply the knowledge, skills, and habits of mind they develop throughout the unit. All the work and learning of the unit builds towards creating the culminating assessment.

• **Reflection and Self-assessment** – This occurs throughout the unit as a part of ongoing assessment and at the end of the unit when students and teachers reflect on the unit to see what worked well and what can be improved.

Selection and Sequence of Learning Experiences

These are how students engage with the content, learn the skills, and develop the habits of mind that are the unit's goals. The sequence of activities should be designed to move students towards achieving the learning goals and creating the culminating assessment.

An academic-based course curriculum is designed to provide students with the knowledge and skills they need to succeed in their academic studies and future careers. It refers to educational content and instruction based on a specific academic subject or field of study.

It is designed to meet the learning standards and objectives set by educational institutions, such as schools, colleges, or universities, and typically includes a variety of different types of content, such as textbook readings, lectures, assignments, and assessments, designed to help students learn and understand key concepts and develop the knowledge, skills, and critical thinking abilities in a particular subject area.

An academic-based curriculum is often organized into different levels, such as elementary, middle, and high school, or undergraduate and graduate levels, and is often developed by educational experts and professionals, such as teachers, professors, and curriculum developers. It is based on research and evidence-based practices and is continually reviewed and updated to remain current and relevant.

An academic-based curriculum differs from a vocational or technical curriculum, which focuses on teaching students skills and knowledge directly applicable to a specific occupation or trade in that it is designed to provide students with a broad and deep understanding of a subject area.

Experience/Expert-based Curriculum

This type of curriculum emphasizes the complex outcomes of a learning process, that is, the knowledge, skills, and attitudes to be applied by learners rather than mainly focusing on what learners are expected to learn about in terms of traditionally defined subject content.

In principle, such a curriculum is learner-centered and adaptive to the changing needs of students, teachers, and society. It implies that learning activities and environments are chosen so that learners can acquire and apply the knowledge, skills, and attitudes to situations they encounter in everyday life.

Experience-based curricula are usually designed around key competencies that can be cross-curricular and subject-bound. The distinguishing feature of experience-based curricula (or experiential curricula) is that they cater to the experience of the learners, which occupies a central place in all considerations of teaching and learning.

These experiences may comprise earlier events in the learner's life, current life events, or experiences arising from the learner's participation in activities implemented by teachers and facilitators. A key element of an experience-based curriculum is that it will enable learners to analyze their experience by reflecting, evaluating, and reconstructing that experience (sometimes individually, sometimes collectively, sometimes both) to draw meaning from it in the light of prior experience.

This review of their experience may lead to further action.

All learning necessarily involves experience of some sort, whether prior and/or current. However, observing many contemporary teaching and training practices might lead one to think otherwise. Much of the impetus for the experience-based curriculum has been a reaction against an approach to learning that is didactic, teacher-driven, and involves a discipline-focused transmission of knowledge.

It supports a more participative, learner-centered approach, which emphasizes personal experience, rich learning events, and the construction of meaning by learners. Experience-based learning is particularly interesting to adult educators because it encompasses formal, informal, non-formal, life, incidental, and workplace learning.

According to Boud, Cohen, and Walker 1993, an experience-based curriculum is based on a set of assumptions about learning from experience. These have been identified as:

- Experience as the foundation of, and the stimulus for, learning

- Learners actively constructing their own experience

- Learning as a holistic process

- Learning as a socially and culturally constructed process and

- Learning is influenced by the socio-emotional context in which it occurs

Whether or not teaching and learning activities are arranged in the forms that are commonly associated with experience-based curricula, these considerations will still apply.

The Defining Characteristics

The defining characteristics of experience-based learning do not lend themselves to being reduced to a set of strategies, methods, formulas, or recipes. It is possible, however, to describe this by recognizing a set of key features that characterize and distinguish it from other approaches.

The first three (whole person, prior experiences, and reflection on experience) probably apply to all experience-based learning. The remaining three (structure of experience, facilitation, and assessment) may or may not be present in any particular case.

The following features can be further explained thus: the involvement of the whole person, i.e., intellect, feelings, and senses. In learning through role-play and games, playing or acting in these typically involves the intellect, some or other of the senses, and a variety of feelings.

Active Use of Life Experiences

Learning occurs through all of these, the recognition and active use of all the learner's relevant life experiences and learning experiences. Where new learning can be related to personal experiences, the meaning thus derived is likely to be more effectively integrated into the learner's values and understanding, the continued reflection upon earlier experiences to add to and transform them into deeper understanding. This process lasts as long as the learner lives and has memory access.

Advocate Learning

Experience-based curricula advocate for the belief that the quality of reflective thought that the learner brings to any experience is of greater significance to the eventual learning outcomes than the nature of the experience itself. Learning is the process whereby knowledge is created through the transformation of experience, whether or not the activity that leads to learning has been intentionally designed for that purpose.

Deliberately Designed

Deliberately designed learning events are often referred to as 'structured' activities and include simulations, games, role-play, visualizations, focus group discussions, socio-drama, and hypotheticals, whether or not the learner's engagement in the experience is facilitated by some other person/s (teachers, leaders, coaches, therapists) and, if it is, the degree of skill with which that facilitation is carried out.

Equality

An experience-based curriculum often assumes relatively equal relationships between facilitator and learner, involves the possibility of negotiation, and gives the learner considerable control and autonomy and whether or not the outcomes of learning through experience are to be assessed and, if so, by what means, by whom, and for what purpose. An experience-based curriculum is often as concerned with the process as the learning outcomes, and the assessment procedures should align with this.

Assessment Tasks

Assessment tasks consistent with the experience-based curriculum include individual or group projects, critical essays in the learner's own experience, reading logs, learning journals, negotiated learning contracts, peer assessment, and self-assessment. They might include a range of presentation modes other than writing to enable the holism, context, and complexity of the learning to be evidenced.

Process of Experience-Based Curriculum

An experience-based curriculum embraces experience-based learning, which is not just a mere 'method' or 'technique' or even a particular 'approach'; it is as wide and deep as education itself.

Although there is no single way to identify the experience-based learning process, some criteria must be fulfilled if teaching and learning activities are labeled 'experience-based.'

Ends of Education

The most important primary criterion refers to the 'ends' of education: its goals, purposes, and what it is trying to achieve. One must follow that with several criteria that refer to the means of education; that is, how we do things to achieve those goals or ends. Experience-based learning is a well-known approach to education that primarily focuses on the student's demonstration of their desired learning outcomes as central to the overall learning process.

It is largely based on the premise of a student's progression through the curriculum (as their competencies are proven) at their own speed, pace, depth, and other similar parameters.

Competency-Based Learning with Experience

Rather than just focusing on what learners are expected to learn in terms of traditionally defined subject content, a competency-based curriculum emphasizes the various complex outcomes of a learning process, such as the skills, knowledge, and attitudes to be applied by learners.

Some of the benefits of competency-based learning are that its approach is flexible as learners can move at their own pace; it supports students with diverse literacy levels, knowledge backgrounds, and other related aptitudes, and with it, students are far better prepared with the necessary skills to succeed as adults; and it allows students to take responsibility for their education.

Designing an experience-based curriculum mainly concerns creating varied opportunities for students that allow them to demonstrate important skills in authentic contexts.

Identify and Map

The first step in this development is to identify and map the general competency areas using a wide range of sources of information and techniques to collect them. These competencies offer a framework based on specific performance outcomes to develop a curriculum and measure performance. The sources used can include subject matter experts, high-performing students, educators, online textbooks, and articles.

The techniques that can be used include focus groups, surveys, readings, and observations. Although each student has their own unique set of competencies, these competency maps are generally created by observing and interviewing top-performing students to capture their performance as a list of core competencies (knowledge and abilities).

Specific Competencies

In the next step, you must define specific competencies in each general area. Developing an accurate and precise description will make the next steps much easier in curriculum development. To fully define a competency, reflect thoroughly on its composing elements. For instance, consider both delivery (body language, voice) and content (language, persuasion, organization) for public speaking. At this point, consider the following questions to help frame your goals around a competency-based curriculum.

- What are the broad advantages of competency-based learning, and why are these important?

- What are the specific benefits it can offer your institution/online teaching platform?

- What are some of the unique goals of your institution around/online teaching platform?

- How will you measure the success of this initiative for your institution/online teaching platform?

- What is the content required to support the development of the specific competency in the curriculum?

- And, what are the instructional strategies and methods that are most effective in developing the competency?

For each of the competencies, establish criteria for performance, that is, create the standards or rubrics by which you can measure the competence. Make sure to describe several levels that define positive and negative competence at this step. This will help you gauge the effectiveness of the curriculum and determine what works well and what doesn't for the learners.

Once you have defined competencies and criteria for outcomes, create learning experiences and think about how students will demonstrate these skills via learning experiences. There are multiple ways to demonstrate these skills, so make sure that the products of the assessment, that is, the student's work, are varied and interesting.

Recognizing

The ideal way to recognize a competency-based learning experience is to thoroughly look at the work the students produce and the learning environment in which they produce it. For instance, teachers and students regularly use the identified competencies and outcomes to reflect on learning.

The idea here is to empower students to be real learning designers. Allow them to use the rubric to design a learning experience where they can demonstrate the learning outcomes and give them the responsibility of the planning, execution, and presentation of their work for assessment.

Assessing

A successful competency-based curriculum will enable students to apply and execute the knowledge, skills, and abilities the industry desires. To bridge this gap between industry and academia, there is a need for a structured process of connecting knowledge, skills, and abilities to assessment.

When assessing competencies, you need to address two important questions:

Have the students acquired the specified competencies by the end of the program?

If yes, was this acquisition of the competencies a result of the program?

You need various assessment methods here for assessing the program-level competencies, including formative and summative assessments and self-assessment.

Be Prepared for Change

As the curriculum gets implemented and students begin to develop competence in various areas, there will be a lot of likely changes. It is, therefore, important to evaluate the curriculum's efficacy to deliver competence, refine it to meet the desired goals better, and then repeat the process to ensure ongoing effectiveness.

Students learn best when their school experience or their instructor's experience is connected to real life. The skills-based curriculum focuses on equipping students with the required knowledge and appropriate life skills. This curriculum gives each student an equal opportunity to master the necessary skills and become a successful adult.

In basic terms, experience-based curriculum/education means that, instead of focusing on grades and yearly curriculum schedules, the main focus is placed on how competent each student is in the subject. This means that students can only move forward when they can demonstrate mastery.

Personalizing

Experience-based curriculum/education and personalized learning go hand-in-hand. By personalizing the learning experience for each student, teachers ensure that each student has full mastery before they can progress. This way, the goal of equity is achieved. That is, students move forward at their own pace, but everyone in the class achieves mastery. The experience-based curriculum clearly focuses on preparing students for the next stage of their life, whether it be college or a career.

A relatively modern approach to learning design, the experience-based curriculum is gaining rapid popularity among educational institutions since it shows a definite improvement in job-oriented skills for students.

By identifying the skills, knowledge, and abilities necessary for achieving success in any industry or occupation the students choose to pursue, the approach can be used to develop and evaluate an experience-based curriculum. It ensures students are better prepared to face work-related challenges later in life. Apart from helping students develop and demonstrate mastery over a topic, an experience-based curriculum builds a culture of equity and inclusivity and adequately prepares students for life.

Summary

An experience-based curriculum emphasizes the complex learning process outcomes, such as knowledge, skills, and attitudes, rather than just focusing on traditional subject content. It is learner-centered and adapts to the changing needs of students, teachers, and society. It is designed around a set of core competencies/competencies that can be cross-curricular and subject-bound.

Moreover, it is designed around the learners' experiences, which occupy a central place in all teaching and learning considerations. These experiences may include past events in the life of the learners, current life events, or experiences arising from their participation in activities implemented by teachers and facilitators.

A key element of an experience-based curriculum is that it enables learners to analyze their experiences by reflecting, evaluating, and reconstructing that experience, either individually, collectively, or both, to draw meaning from it in light of prior experience. This review of their experience may lead to further action.

In summary, an experience-based curriculum focuses on the learner's experience and emphasizes acquiring and applying knowledge, skills, and attitudes to real-life situations. It is adaptive, learner-centered, and designed to support the development of key competencies that can be applied across subjects and contexts.

It is also designed to allow learners to reflect on their experiences and evaluate and reconstruct them to gain a deeper understanding.

Scheme of Work

A scheme of work is a vital tool in education, providing a detailed, logical, and sequential plan that interprets the syllabus into manageable units for teaching in a structured manner. It serves as a roadmap for educators, outlining the topics to be covered within a specific timeframe, whether a week, a month, a term, or even an entire year.

This comprehensive plan plays a crucial role in the teaching-learning process and offers several significant benefits:

1. **Systematic and Orderly Teaching:** One of the fundamental functions of a scheme of work is to ensure that topics in the syllabus are taught logically and systematically. It guides teachers to start with simpler concepts and progress to more complex ones, enhancing students' understanding and learning outcomes.

2. **Comprehensive Coverage:** By breaking down the syllabus into manageable units, the scheme of work ensures that every topic is covered, leaving no gaps in students' knowledge and comprehension of the subject matter.

3. **Time Management:** Effective time management is crucial in education, and a scheme of work helps teachers budget their time wisely. It accounts for potential disruptions in the school

calendar, such as public holidays, prize-giving days, and sports events, allowing instructors to plan their lessons accordingly.

4. **Preparation and Insight:** The scheme of work provides teachers with valuable insight into their teaching. It allows them to identify the content, methods, and relevant instructional materials they will use in each lesson, giving them ample time to prepare adequately.

5. **Guiding Lesson Planning:** A well-designed scheme of work becomes a foundation for creating detailed lesson plans. Teachers can use it to guide their daily or weekly teaching, ensuring they cover all the necessary topics and learning objectives.

6. **Pace of Teaching:** The scheme of work helps educators gauge their pace of teaching. It ensures that they progress through the curriculum appropriately, neither rushing through topics nor lagging behind.

7. **Continuity in Learning:** The scheme of work becomes particularly valuable during teacher transitions. When a teacher is transferred, the incoming educator can seamlessly take over from where the previous one left off, ensuring continuity in the learning process without repetition or omission.

The structure of a scheme of work revolves around how the curriculum will be taught. It involves the order of lessons, allocating teaching hours to each topic, and incorporating any assessment activities deemed necessary. Teachers use the scheme of work to plan and sequence their lessons in advance, ensuring that all course content is covered within the designated timeframe and curriculum aims are met.

Furthermore, a well-designed scheme of work encourages teachers to consider and utilize the available resources to their advantage. These teaching resources, ranging from multimedia presentations to activity sheets, engage students in learning. Educators can effectively assess their resources by organizing lessons beforehand and identifying any additional materials needed.

An essential aspect of a scheme of work is mapping out how resources, class activities, and assessment strategies will be used to teach each topic and evaluate students' progress. This comprehensive approach helps students recognize the interconnections between different topics and units as they progress through the course.

The scheme of work is usually an interpretation of the curriculum's specification or syllabus, acting as a guide throughout the course to monitor progress against the original plan. Students can also benefit from access to the scheme of work, as it provides an overview of their course, making it easier to follow the curriculum's structure.

The government defines the ultimate source of the curriculum through laws and regulations. Each country has its own curricula, although some may adopt curricula defined by other nations. Therefore, aligning it with the legally required curriculum of the country where it will be implemented is essential when generating a scheme of work. A deep understanding of the subtleties and nuances of the curriculum's presentation is crucial in defining the most useful schemes of work.

A well-prepared scheme of work should offer an overview of the total course content, a sequential listing of learning tasks, a relationship between content and support materials, and a basis for long-range planning, training, and course evaluation.

A scheme of work is a fundamental educational tool that enables teachers to teach systematically and in an orderly way, ensuring comprehensive syllabus coverage. It facilitates efficient time management and preparation guides lesson planning, and aids in monitoring the pace of teaching.

Moreover, it promotes continuity in learning during teacher transitions, supporting a seamless learning process for students. By aligning with the curriculum's goals and incorporating available resources, a well-designed scheme of work becomes a roadmap for educators to navigate the teaching-learning journey successfully.

Key Considerations for Preparing a Scheme of Work:

Understanding the Syllabus

The classroom teacher may not necessarily be involved in the initial stages of curriculum development but is expected to interpret and implement the curriculum correctly. This calls for a thorough understanding of the syllabus and the content to achieve the stated objectives.

The teacher is expected to act like a police officer or judge called upon to administer the law, though they did not make it. Therefore, the teacher must be thoroughly conversant with the curriculum to implement it successfully.

Preceding and Succeeding Syllabus Content

In most cases, topics from the syllabus may not be arranged in the order they are supposed to be taught. Some topics will require knowledge of the previous ones, while others are quite independent. The teacher should identify the essential learning content but also arrange the content in logical teaching order considering the proceeding and succeeding syllabus content.

Syllabus contents of the related subject – the mistake many teachers make is to scheme for their subject without considering the contents of related subjects. I'm afraid that's not right and should be highly discouraged. Quite often, teaching a given topic in a given subject may be impeded by a lack of skills or knowledge to be acquired in a different subject.

The Existing Scheme of Work for the Subject

If a scheme of work is already available for the subject, it would be a waste of effort and time for the teacher to break new ground again. In this case, the teacher can revise the existing scheme to suit their students and keep it current.

Reference Material and Examination

The teacher should be familiar with available reference material for effective coverage of the topics in the scheme of work. Nothing is more disturbing than discovering that a topic already covered could have been more interesting, enjoyable, and even better understood if certain materials or teaching aids available in school had been utilized.

The type of examination the students are being prepared for should bear consideration that some levels require more revision time than others and, therefore, scheme for revision appropriately.

Time Estimation

Although there is a given time of weeks in one term, it is not usually possible to use all these for effective teaching for various reasons. To determine how much material can be covered at any given time, it would be misleading to assume that a subject requires certain periods per week available for teaching.

The number of effective teaching periods varies according to both predictable and unpredictable interruptions. Effective teaching time must hence be estimated before topics are selected.

The most common interruptions to disrupt a scheme of work include:

- Public holidays

- Examinations (should be schemed for) if they are internal

- Revisions (should be schemed for)

- Open days

- Sports days

- Planned school breaks, e.g., mid-term break

Before scheming, the teacher/instructor should check with the school administration for the dates of such events. Finer adjustments need to be made depending on the time available for teaching.

Key Components of Scheme of Work

Organization: The organization/institution one is working or training in.

Trainee Level: The grade level in training, e.g., technician. In the case of colleges and other institutions, some means of identification can be used.

Subject: The subject being schemed, which may be theory or practical, refers to a particular term within a given year. Years may vary from organization to organization, depending on the time of entry.

Date of Preparation: The time the scheme of work is completed. This should be before instruction commences.

Date of Revision: Due to overlapping or under-planning experienced during instruction or unforeseen interruptions; it can be necessary to revise the scheme of work to accommodate unexpected difficulties. This date should be indicated in the space provided in the form.

Syllabus Topics: These need to be arranged in the order they are supposed to be taught. This is because some topics are built up, e.g., before one learns to multiply, they should have made additions, etc. The syllabus topics should then follow that order.

Week: Most organizations are specific in time allocation, and each week should be spelled out in the week column. The week's numeral should be distinctly written centrally in the week column. Weeks should be separated by a line running across the page, especially when the same scheme of work form contains more than one week.

Number of Periods: The subject may have one, two, or more periods in one week. Some periods may be single, double, or triple. The numbering of the period can take the form of either an ordinal or cardinal system. Ordinal systems refer to the order in which periods for that subject appear on the timetable. In either system, the numbering should be done as reflected on the timetable for that subject.

A line, beginning from the column of periods, should be drawn straight across the page to separate the periods. When two-spaced periods are indicated on the timetable on the same day, there should be two distinct rows. The numbering process should be repeated for the other weeks.

Date When Taught: The actual date when the topic or activity is taught in class. It helps to keep track of the progress of the course and ensure that all topics are covered within the allocated time frame. It is important to update this column regularly and make any necessary adjustments to the schedule if needed.

Sub-topic/lesson Titles: This should be clear and definite. The instructor should list all the sub-topics/lesson titles in a particular syllabus topic. They should then estimate what sub-topics/lesson titles will require a single, double, or triple period and then plan accordingly.

Objectives: Each sub-topic/lesson title should be followed by an objective(s), which is meant to pinpoint the anticipated learning behavior of the learners. The specific nature of the sub-topic/lesson titles does not permit broad objectives that might not be realized by the end of that period. The objectives must be stated in such a manner that there is a measurable aspect manifested by the end of the lesson, e.g., the lesson title 'Simple interest' might have the objective: *'Students should be able to calculate simple interest on given principals using methods of (i) direct production and (ii) simple interest formula'*; and the lesson title *'Conduction of heat in metals'* might have the objective: *'Trainees will be able to classify good and bad conductors of heat after carrying out the experiment, described in worksheet 4.'*

Key Points/methods: The teacher anticipated using central ideas during the lesson. They are an elaboration of the sub-topic/lesson title and form the backbone of the lesson. Key points should be stated in a specific, precise manner, preferably in phrases that convey the intended meaning. Under no circumstances should key points be stated as activities or activities in a sense.

Application of Scheme of Work

Student Activities, Assignments, Homework, Practice, Etc.

For any concept learned, the teacher wants to see their learners put it to practical use. In this section, the teacher should think of specific activities that the learners will perform while in the class and for homework; for example, students will answer comprehension questions after reading the passage in their textbook, etc. Applications must be designed to realize and concretely consolidate the lesson's objectives.

Tools, Equipment, Apparatus, Chalkboard, Chart, Etc.

Resource materials for specific content coverage used in scheming are necessary and should be noted with their relevant pages for ease of reference during lesson planning. References include books, handouts, worksheets, journals, reports, etc. The teacher must indicate the books, their authors, and the relevant pages.

Teaching aids are an integral part of an effective lesson. Aids that the teacher intends to use should be indicated in the scheme of work. Teaching aids are usually in the form of apparatus, equipment, materials, and, of course, the real thing if readily available and appropriate. The teacher should not indicate a teaching aid that will not be available in class.

Note: Most teachers forget to include teaching aids in the scheme of work.

Remarks: Remarks in the scheme of work should be made immediately after the lesson. The teacher is supposed to indicate whether what was planned for the period has been covered, whether there was over-planning or failure of the lesson, and reasons for either case, etc. Remarks suggested are meant to help the teacher in their consequent and future planning.

Remarks such as 'excellently done,' 'okay,' 'well done,' 'satisfactory,' and 'taught' might not be very valuable to the teacher. Such remarks as 'the lesson was not very well done because of inadequate teaching aids' or 'pupils could apply concepts learned in solving problems as evident from supervised practice' are appropriate. After the remarks, it is necessary to write the date when this lesson was taught.

Summary

A scheme of work is a detailed plan that breaks down a syllabus into manageable units that can be covered in a specific period. It ensures that topics in the syllabus are taught orderly, from the simplest to the most complex.

It helps teachers to budget for time wisely, giving room for events and activities that might interfere with the school/college/university calendar. It also guides the teacher in making a lesson plan, checking the teacher's pace of teaching, and ensuring continuity in the learning process when a teacher is transferred.

It also helps teachers to consider and make the most of the resources at their disposal and to plan and sequence their lessons in advance. Schemes of work should also align with the legally required curricula of the country.

The components of a scheme of work should be observed because they are essential for effective planning and instruction. In addition, the components help teachers to consider and exploit the resources at their disposal and to plan and sequence their lessons in advance. This helps to ensure that all course content is taught before the school year ends and that the curriculum aims are covered.

The components also help to ensure that the learning objectives are met and that the students are engaged in the learning process. The objectives, key points, and methods help teachers plan lessons and deliver the content meaningfully and effectively. The student activities, assignments, homework, and practice help to ensure that the students are actively engaged in the learning process and can apply what they have learned to real-world situations.

Overall, observing the components of a scheme of work helps to ensure that the instruction is well-organized, well-planned, and effective in helping students achieve the desired learning outcomes.

Chapter 9: Online Teaching Software

The landscape of distance learning has evolved from its earlier incarnations, ushering in significant advancements largely attributable to the internet's capabilities. These improvements encompass robust communication tools and a wealth of information that continues to expand, readily accessible through limitless communication channels. Therefore, selecting an appropriate online learning platform is crucial to ensure effective training delivery.

As an online education provider, your goal is to fulfill your responsibilities, accomplish your work, and generate income from the comfort of your own space. It is imperative to opt for a user-friendly and transparent platform. Even if you encounter misunderstandings or complexities, having access to a responsive support team that can promptly offer solutions is invaluable.

Before hastily investing in your first online training software, take a moment to consider your specific needs. Engage key stakeholders in discussions about the "why," "how," and "what" of your current online training offerings. If you're starting from scratch, outline your non-negotiable requirements and desired features.

If you are already teaching, evaluate what aspects are functioning well in your current training programs and what needs improvement. Identify the features you want your online training software to encompass. Clarifying your expectations and priorities from the outset will enable you to make a well-informed decision.

Selecting the Right Online Training Software

Here are a few key factors to consider when choosing online training software:

Audience Consideration

Always begin by considering the end-users. The ideal online teaching platform should be intuitive and straightforward for teachers, students, and administrators. Customizing educational materials and making them accessible to learners should pose no difficulties. Ensure the platform offers intuitive interfaces, clear controls, and robust support options as essential selection criteria.

Identifying Necessary Online Learning Features

Pay significant attention to determining the essential features required to facilitate effective teaching. Define your preferred teaching style and consider which solutions align with your needs. If you're not tech-savvy, consult with experienced companies specializing in similar solutions to guide your selection.

Focus on Accessibility in Education

Accessibility extends beyond the devices used by trainers and learners. Providing content that is accessible to the target audience greatly enhances the overall educational process. Ensure that quality and features remain consistent across laptops, smartphones, and tablets. Simplify online classes to minimize effort for participants. Consider incorporating assessment items like graphs and tables, emphasizing key ideas. Remember that less can often be more in digital learning. Select a platform that is comfortable and accessible for all, incorporating texts, visuals, icons, colors, and user-friendly design elements.

Prioritize Security

Security is paramount for online teaching platforms, whether for schools or individual educators. Prioritize security measures to safeguard both educators and students. This security ensures peace of mind and compliance with data protection regulations.

Consider using a Virtual Private Network (VPN) to establish a secure connection, encrypting your data traffic and concealing your IP address. This safeguards your online activities from external threats.

Protect valuable content, such as video courses or private live training, by restricting access until purchase. Additionally, secure live training sessions to prevent unauthorized entry. Select a platform prioritizing students' personal information security and providing reliable servers.

Streamlined User Experience

An efficient online teaching platform should offer a seamless user experience. Ensure all buttons, icons, and links function properly, guiding users to the necessary pages without glitches. A user-friendly interface can significantly enhance the teaching and learning process.

Scalability and Flexibility

Anticipate future growth and changing needs. Choose a platform that can scale with you and hopefully your new start-up and adapt to evolving educational requirements. Flexibility in terms of adding new features or modules can be invaluable as your educational offerings expand.

Integration Capabilities

Consider how well the chosen software integrates with your existing systems and tools if you have one.

Seamless integration with Learning Management Systems (LMS), content management systems, and other educational technology can simplify administrative tasks and enhance the overall learning experience.

Cost-Effectiveness

While considering all the essential features and functionalities, also assess the cost-effectiveness of the online training software. Ensure that it aligns with your budgetary constraints and offers a good return on investment in terms of improved training outcomes.

User Support and Training

Evaluate the support and training options provided by the software provider. Effective onboarding and ongoing support can significantly impact your ability to utilize the platform to its fullest potential. Look for platforms that offer training resources, tutorials, and responsive customer support.

Reviews and Recommendations

Research and read reviews from other educators or institutions using the platform. Recommendations from trusted sources can provide valuable insights into the software's performance, reliability, and suitability for your specific educational goals.

User Feedback and Iteration

After implementing your chosen online training software, actively seek teacher and student feedback. Their input can reveal areas that need improvement and inform future iterations of your online teaching platform. An adaptive software enhancement approach can align your educational offerings with evolving needs.

Data Analytics and Reporting

Look for a platform that provides robust data analytics and reporting capabilities. Data-driven insights can help you track student progress, identify areas of improvement, and tailor your teaching methods accordingly. Comprehensive analytics can be a valuable tool for continuous improvement in your educational programs.

Accessibility Compliance

Ensure the online training software adheres to accessibility standards and regulations, such as WCAG (Web Content Accessibility Guidelines). This is crucial for accommodating learners with disabilities and promoting inclusivity in your online courses.

Content Management

Evaluate the content management capabilities of the platform. Efficient content creation, organization, and updating are essential for delivering engaging and up-to-date educational materials. Features like version control and content reuse can streamline this process.

Collaboration Features

Consider whether the software offers collaboration features such as discussion boards, chat functionality, and group projects. These tools can foster a sense of community and active student engagement, enhancing the online learning experience.

Regular Software Updates

Opt for a platform that regularly updates its software to stay current with technological advancements and security measures. Frequent updates ensure that your online teaching environment remains reliable and secure.

Trial Period

Before committing to a long-term contract, take advantage of any trial or demo periods the software provider offers. This allows you to explore the platform's features and gauge its suitability for your specific needs without financial commitment.

Long-Term Viability

Consider the long-term viability of the software provider. Choose a company with a solid track record and a commitment to ongoing development and support. This minimizes the risk of being left with outdated software in the future.

Widely Used Features to Consider

In the current landscape of technological advancements, you have a wide array of features and solutions to choose from. You don't need to be a subject-specific teacher to benefit from various functional features. The most commonly employed features to consider are:

Video Courses

Perhaps the most ubiquitous feature online education providers utilize is the ability to create and publish online video courses. This allows you to develop and share content on your platform, making it accessible for sale. Online video courses offer convenience to your audience, enabling them to receive education from the comfort of their preferred environment and at their convenience. On the other hand, educators put in the effort upfront by recording, editing, and publishing courses, but the income continues to flow each time learners purchase the course.

Live Calls and Automated Live Training

At certain junctures in online education, real-time, face-to-face communication becomes necessary. Live calls serve as an ideal medium for interacting with learners. Additionally, you can organize automated live training sessions. For example, this might entail a monthly training program encompassing three weekly lessons. To facilitate this, you'll require features that allow you to schedule lessons, create timetables, introduce topics, provide brief descriptions, and inform the audience about the subjects covered in each lesson. This feature also streamlines the process of inviting students; you won't need to individually contact each student as they will receive automated email notifications with all the requisite details.

Quizzes and Tests

Education is incomplete without assessments. Learners seek to test their acquired knowledge and evaluate their progress. As an education provider, it's essential to meet these requirements effectively. The online quiz feature can automate the test-checking process. When setting up quizzes, you can specify correct answers for questions, and the system will automatically calculate results when students complete the tests. These quizzes can encompass various question formats, including short or long answers, yes or no responses, and multiple-choice questions. In some instances, you can even incorporate videos or attach images to provide context to questions or answer choices.

Certification

Students who successfully pass tests with positive marks often desire certificates to validate their acquired knowledge and skills. You certainly wouldn't want to disappoint them. Therefore, it is highly recommended to include this feature. Linking the test and certification features can streamline your work further. When students achieve passing grades, the system can automatically generate certificates bearing the student's name and results. In today's educational landscape, students value this function greatly, as they aspire to earn certifications and showcase them on their CVs.

Student Engagement Tools

To create an interactive and engaging learning experience, consider features that facilitate student interaction. Forums, discussion boards, chat rooms, and collaborative projects are excellent tools to encourage communication among learners. These features can foster a sense of community and peer-to-peer learning, enhancing the overall educational journey.

Progress Tracking and Analytics

Implement features that allow both educators and students to track progress and performance. This can include personalized dashboards displaying course progress, grades, and completion status. Comprehensive analytics can provide insights into individual and class-wide performance, helping the learners identify areas that may require additional attention or modification.

Personalization and Customization

Look for features that enable personalized learning experiences. Tailoring content and assignments to individual student needs can significantly enhance engagement and comprehension. Features such as adaptive learning algorithms, personalized recommendations, and customizable course content can contribute to a more effective educational environment.

Feedback and Communication Channels

Effective communication is essential in online education. Features for providing feedback on assignments, answering student inquiries, and conducting one-on-one discussions are crucial. Ensure your chosen platform offers communication tools that facilitate prompt and clear interactions between educators and students.

Mobile Compatibility

In an increasingly mobile world, ensure the platform is mobile-friendly and compatible with various devices and screen sizes. This allows learners to access course materials on smartphones and tablets, providing flexibility and accessibility.

Technical Support and Training Resources

Evaluate the technical support and training resources offered by the platform provider. Effective onboarding and ongoing support can alleviate issues and maximize the platform's utility. Look for platforms that provide documentation, tutorials, and responsive customer support to assist educators and students.

Scalability and Integration

Consider the scalability of the platform to accommodate future growth. Additionally, assess its ability to integrate with other educational tools and systems, such as Learning Management Systems (LMS) or content management platforms. Seamless integration can streamline administrative tasks and enhance the overall learning experience.

Cost Analysis and Budgeting

While exploring features, keep your budget in mind. Carefully assess the costs associated with the platform and ensure it aligns with your financial resources. Consider not only the initial setup costs but also ongoing maintenance and licensing fees.

Self Analysis

This is necessary to enhance the effectiveness of the educational process, address issues, and improve overall quality. It is essential to conduct a thorough analysis of user behavior on your chosen platform. This analysis will help identify points of confusion and features that users may find unfavorable. Analytical reports will furnish you with the necessary information for efficient process management.

When selecting an online teaching platform, it is equally important to consider the availability of analytics. This capability enables you to, for example, determine whether students are watching and completing all assigned videos. Are there specific content segments that tend to disengage students or necessitate repeated viewing? The analytical features integrated into your online learning platform will aid in refining both individual classes and the overall virtual learning experience. Additionally, these features can provide instructors with essential data to assess student performance and offer targeted support as needed.

Naturally, you may require additional features and functionalities to facilitate specific teaching activities. Consequently, it is prudent to assess the availability of these features. Furthermore, you should compare the costs associated with these features to identify an affordable option that aligns with your desired capabilities.

Criteria for Learning Platforms

When choosing online learning platforms, it's important to consider the following factors:

- Age
- Socio-cultural characteristics
- Internet usage skills
- Educational needs
- Type of course
- Number of students
- Course methodology
- Server hardware and software requirements
- Maximum number of concurrent online users
- Security and access control
- Technological infrastructure requirements
- Necessary technical knowledge
- Platform usability and design strategies.

Your chosen online learning platform should align with the teaching and learning processes, which encompass:

- **Methodology:** Teacher's teaching methodology and student's learning methodology.

- **Type of content to be taught:** Including content indexing, glossaries, content search tools, support for various content formats, multimedia capabilities, offline access options, and evaluation of the teaching/learning process, including initial assessment.

- **Formative or continuous evaluation:** Tools for tracking student activities, observation and monitoring, and self-evaluation tools for students.

- **Summative evaluation:** Including various types of tests (multiple-choice, matching, fill in the blanks, short and open-ended responses), student support systems, course design tools, and communication tools that facilitate teacher-student interaction and collaborative work.

Communication tools should support both asynchronous and synchronous interaction:

- **Asynchronous:** Discussion forums, distribution lists, electronic mail, tutorials, notice boards, and calendars.

- **Synchronous:** Shared electronic board, chat, audio conference, videoconference.

While it's crucial to recognize that online learning encompasses more than just technology, it's equally vital to analyze and evaluate the learning process to understand learners' demands, preferences, and actions comprehensively. The selection of a suitable online learning platform serves as a fundamental prerequisite. An effective online learning platform must address the diversity of learning needs on a global scale, acknowledging learners' wide-ranging characteristics and requirements.

The Importance of a Robust Training and Training Management Solution

Effective training is essential for attracting and retaining a substantial number of students. An efficient online training program can transform individuals into high performers in less time than it would take to recruit and hire them individually.

A robust training management solution plays a pivotal role in creating, delivering, and tracking employee training programs. When integrated with policy and accreditation management solutions, your organization can operate seamlessly on all fronts.

Selecting training management software that aligns with your organization's specific needs may seem challenging.

Training and development must be tailored to suit the intended users. Over the years, we've come to understand that people have varying learning styles, speeds, and sensory preferences. Therefore, your online training software should prioritize ease of use and offer the flexibility to upload custom content that caters to diverse learning styles.

Introducing a new digital training management system doesn't necessarily mean starting from scratch or reinventing the wheel. Review the existing training content you have at your disposal, such as PowerPoint presentations, videos, recorded lectures, and established policies and procedures.

Several training management solutions offer pre-packaged training materials for organizations lacking pre-existing training content, specifically tailored to sectors like healthcare, law enforcement, and other regulated industries.

However, creating your own training content is often more effective. After all, no one understands your own needs better than yourself. Customized training content tends to be more engaging and resonates with your corporate culture and organizational requirements. This approach encourages employee engagement and highlights the practical applications of the training in their daily work.

Training software should simplify the training process, not complicate it. If users find the software challenging to navigate, their effectiveness and interest in using it will diminish. Enthusiasm dwindles, and while individuals may reluctantly complete mandatory courses, voluntary participation declines.

Hence, when comparing software options, consider how user-friendly it is:

- Is it intuitive?

- Can everyone easily grasp how to use it?

- What is the initial learning curve like?

- Is it straightforward for even the most tech-resistant staff?

- How user-friendly is the administrative interface?

- Does it facilitate the creation and distribution of custom training?

- Are the tracking tools simple to operate?

- Can you easily generate reports and dashboards?

Choosing a training and training management solution that prioritizes user-friendliness is crucial for ensuring effective and widespread adoption within your organization.

Popular Teaching Platforms for Live Classes

Online classes have become an integral part of modern life, and the choice of platform plays a crucial role in delivering effective online education. Numerous platforms are available for conducting online classes, all geared toward delivering lectures and educational content to students. Let's explore some of the most popular teaching platforms for live classes:

NCH Debut

NCH Debut, developed by NCH Software, is a versatile video capture and screen recording software that empowers users to record video from their webcam, screen, or other input devices. The software supports audio recording and offers video editing capabilities, including cropping, trimming, and color correction.

Notable features of NCH Debut include the ability to record in various formats like MP4, AVI, WMV, and FLV, options for capturing the entire screen or specific areas, and the capability to add captions and text. Users can also schedule recordings in advance and easily upload videos to platforms such as YouTube and Vimeo. NCH Debut is a valuable tool for creating video tutorials and meeting a variety of recording needs, boasting a user-friendly interface and extensive editing options.

OBS Studio (Open Broadcaster Software)

OBS Studio, a free and open-source video recording and live-streaming software, is widely embraced by content creators, educators, and streamers. The software supports multiple sources, including webcam, screen capture, and audio capture, allowing users to arrange and display content flexibly.

It offers recording options in various formats like MP4 and FLV and facilitates live streaming to platforms like YouTube, Twitch, and Facebook. The built-in audio and video mixing feature enables users to adjust levels of different sources, and the software supports various plugins and add-ons to enhance functionality.

OBS Studio's intuitive interface simplifies navigation and customization, making it a versatile and powerful choice for creating high-quality video content.

Loom

Loom is a user-friendly screen recording and video communication tool that streamlines creating and sharing videos for work and education. It enables users to record their screens and webcams and share recordings via links. The software offers options to record the entire screen or specific areas and provides audio recording and captioning features.

Loom's webcam recording feature adds a personal touch to videos, making it well-suited for video tutorials, training, and remote communication. It seamlessly integrates with popular tools like Google Drive, Slack, and Trello, facilitating secure video sharing with team members, clients, and students.

Dropbox Capture

Dropbox Capture, developed by Dropbox, is a screen recording and video capture tool designed for effortless video creation and sharing in professional and educational settings. Users can record their screen, webcam, or audio and share the recordings via links. Similar to Loom, Dropbox Capture offers features for capturing the entire screen or specific areas, adding audio and captions, and recording with the webcam.

The software seamlessly integrates with Dropbox, enabling users to save and share recordings effortlessly. Dropbox Capture is a convenient tool for quickly creating and sharing videos, making it ideal for remote teams, educators, and anyone needing video content creation.

Zoom

Zoom is a widely adopted video conferencing and webinar software that facilitates virtual meetings, online education, and telemedicine. It supports high-quality video and audio, accommodating up to 1,000 participants in a single meeting.

Zoom allows for screen sharing, video playback, and local or cloud-based recording of meetings. It includes features like breakout rooms for group discussions and offers virtual backgrounds to conceal real backgrounds. The software also supports various integrations, providing users with a secure and feature-rich platform for conducting virtual meetings and webinars.

Camtasia

Camtasia, developed by TechSmith, is a versatile screen recording and video editing software. Users can record their screen and webcam and edit the recordings using a range of editing tools. Camtasia supports audio recording, offers a library of royalty-free music and sound effects, and allows for importing and editing existing videos.

The software provides a variety of video effects, including animations, callouts, and transitions, and enables video exports in formats like MP4, WMV, and AVI. It seamlessly integrates with popular platforms such as YouTube, Vimeo, and Screencast.com, making it a powerful tool for creating high-quality video tutorials, marketing videos, and other content.

Vimeo

Vimeo is a video hosting and sharing platform catering to professional video creators and businesses. It offers high-quality video playback and supports various video formats. Users can upload and share videos privately or publicly, and Vimeo provides built-in video editing tools for trimming and editing videos.

The platform offers advanced privacy settings, including password protection and access restrictions. Additionally, users can monetize videos by enabling purchase or rental options. Vimeo also offers advanced analytics to track views, engagement, and other metrics, making it a comprehensive platform for professionals and businesses seeking to share high-quality video content.

Microsoft Teams

Microsoft Teams is a widely adopted online teaching platform commonly utilized across diverse educational settings, including schools, colleges, and coaching institutes. It streamlines online classes with an array of features, including the ability to record live lectures, download recorded sessions, and automatically track attendance. The platform primarily serves as an ideal environment for conducting live lectures and interactive classes, offering an intuitive and user-friendly platform for remote teaching and collaboration.

Summary

Online teaching platforms are a valuable tool for educators to conduct classes remotely and provide a high-quality learning experience for their students. These platforms typically offer a wide range of features designed to mimic the traditional classroom experience and facilitate remote learning.

One of the key features of most online teaching platforms is video conferencing. This allows educators to conduct live lectures and interact with students in real time, just as they would in a traditional classroom setting. Video conferencing also enables educators to use real-time assessments, such as quizzes, polls, and interactive activities, to keep students engaged and active during class.

Another important feature of online teaching platforms is document sharing. This allows educators to share class materials with their students, such as readings, assignments, and presentations. This feature can also provide students access to additional resources, such as videos, articles, and websites relevant to the course.

Interactive tools are also a key feature of online teaching platforms. These tools allow students to engage with each other and the material in various ways, such as through group discussions, collaborative projects, and virtual breakout rooms. These tools also enable educators to create interactive assessments, such as quizzes and exams, which can help to keep students engaged and motivated.

Assessment tools are also a major feature of online teaching platforms. These tools allow educators to track student progress with features such as grade books, analytics, and reports. This allows teachers to monitor student engagement, participation, and academic performance.

This data can be used to identify areas where students may be struggling and adjust teaching methodologies and strategies. Some platforms also allow educators to create automated assessments, such as quizzes, tests, and exams, saving time and resources. Additionally, features like rubrics, feedback, and self-evaluation tools can also be used to help students understand and improve their performance.

Another important aspect of online teaching platforms is communication. These platforms typically offer a variety of ways for educators to communicate with students, such as messaging, email, and forums. This can be used for office hours, discussions, and answering questions. These tools also allow for easy communication between students, fostering a sense of community and collaboration in the class.

Finally, online teaching platforms also offer a variety of administrative features that can assist educators in managing their classes more effectively. For example, some platforms allow educators to create and manage different groups, assign tasks, and schedule online meetings. They also provide access control, analytics, and reporting capabilities, making it easy for educators to monitor and manage student progress, attendance, and participation.

Overall, online teaching platforms are a valuable tool for educators looking to conduct classes remotely and provide a high-quality learning experience for their students. These platforms offer a wide range of features that can help to facilitate remote learning, improve student engagement and performance, and streamline the management of online classes.

Chapter 10: How to Communicate with Greater Clarity, Confidence, and Credibility

Communication is one of the most basic functions of any organization. Communication is essential for achieving managerial and organizational effectiveness. Good communication helps people become more involved in their work and helps them better understand their jobs or roles. Clear, precise, and timely communication of information also prevents the occurrence of organizational problems.

Without communication, people will not be aware of what others are doing, will not have any idea about their goals, and will be unable to assess their performance or that of others. Communicating effectively is crucial for your success in your work and personal life. When you communicate, your listeners must experience you as credible and trustworthy.

They will base this on what you say, how you say it, what they see you doing, and what they think your intent is. Communication is passing information, ideas, knowledge, or feelings from one person to another. Hence, effective communication refers to successfully transferring information from one person to another.

Communication becomes effective when there is an efficient passage of relevant and desirable information, ideas, knowledge, or feelings from one person to another.

Schools are complex, dynamic systems that require effective communication to meet the diverse needs of their stakeholders. Communication is essential to maintaining healthy relationships between students, faculty, and parents.

Components of Effective Communication

Establishing effective communication practices requires understanding communication characteristics, including the benefits and common barriers.

The three critical components of effective communication – trust, transparency, and active listening – build the relationship necessary to engage in challenging conversations and must be established. As a teacher, effective education leadership requires excellent communication skills and a willingness to engage in challenging conversations.

Education platforms, including schools, have many stakeholders: students, teachers, administrators, and families. Each group has high expectations of the educational system, and fulfilling those expectations depends on excellent verbal and non-verbal communication skills.

The benefits and barriers to effective communication must be understood to develop and promote the practice. The characteristics of each stakeholder relationship pose unique challenges and recommendations.

Education contains a variety of unique relationships, each with its own communicative needs and characteristics. The primary relationship in any format, either online or physical school, is at the classroom level.

Communication at this level serves two functions: to support the teacher to meet the learning outcomes and to build a relationship between the participants, namely the students they are teaching. Classrooms must be where students can be vulnerable and know they will be safe. Creating a relationship with students is vital, but that relationship needs to be intellectually based and not focused on building friendships.

Teachers and students have different roles and levels of status, even with open communication and established relationships. Challenging conversations with students, including honest feedback, often begin with the student perceiving the message negatively. The purpose of the discussion is to encourage the students to develop beyond what they feel is possible. Teachers must recognize students' non-verbal communication to understand their thoughts and feelings.

In particular, active listening and emotional intelligence are crucial for identifying and understanding students who have experienced trauma. Establishing and maintaining a classroom with effective communication supports teachers to meet the learning outcomes while creating positive connections.

These skills can be applied to any form of communication: a written research paper, an oral presentation, an online discussion, or speaking with and emailing someone. They can also be applied to a range of professional settings, whether on campus or in the professional world.

The Three C's of Communication

Learning the three C's guidelines can help you be a better communicator. Effective communication requires that the audience understand the message in its intended form.

This comes down to:

- **Clarity** – get to the point!

- **Confidence** – show that you know what you do!

- **Credibility** – do what you know!

Several strategies have been waged by various institutions, business people, or professionals for successful communication in their endeavors, including courtesy, clarity, conciseness, correctness, consideration, and completeness.

Clarity

Clarity means to be clear and is a characteristic of a speech or a prose composition that communicates effectively with its intended audience. In general, the qualities of clearly written prose include a carefully defined purpose, logical organization, well-constructed sentences, and precise word choice. As a teacher or facilitator, you should not mumble.

Enunciate clearly and speak loud enough to be heard. Don't speak too quickly. Use simple language and speak naturally without excessive pauses. Stay on topic. Eliminate distractions. Get feedback.

To achieve clarity, you should choose simple and familiar words, be precise, use appropriate words and phrases, use short sentences, and choose a reasonable speed.

Teacher clarity is an important component of teacher effectiveness. Clarity in instruction enhances students' cognitive learning. An instructor perceived as clear and understandable by their students is also perceived as nonverbally immediate, assertive, and responsive.

At this point, it is assumed that immediate, assertive, and responsive communication behaviors lead to perceptions of greater teacher clarity.

Conciseness

Conciseness is communicating complete information about a topic or idea in a few words. Concise writing also involves being mindful of word choice. Limiting your word count isn't sufficient to write concisely. You need to choose the strongest words to illustrate your point.

However, wordiness is an easy habit to fall into. Some writers write how they speak, using filler phrases and redundant words that might sound natural during the writing process. These unnecessary words can make your written message harder to understand. Concise writing removes or replaces filler, repetitive, and purposeless words from sentences. You can edit your writing for conciseness in several ways.

You should avoid the passive voice. The latter might make sense if you're writing something formal, but sentences with passive voice use more words than active voice. Find the areas of passive voice in the text and recast them into active voice using powerful words.

It would help if you also replaced commonly used phrases. Replacing overused phrases with substantive words is another way to write more concisely. In addition to writing succinctly, your writing has a greater impact because of your deliberate word choices.

You should remove redundant pairs. Some common phrases use two words that have similar meanings. To practice conciseness, choose the strongest one from the pair and remove the weaker. Doing so removes at least one unnecessary word from your writing.

You should remove qualifiers. Qualifiers either amplify or reduce the intensity of another word, but they can lead to wordiness. Aside from conciseness issues, qualifiers that limit a word's impact can also appear unsure and compromise your credibility.

Scan through your writing and remove qualifiers that don't serve a purpose.

Don't ramble or be repetitive.

Eliminate 'uh, uh' between sentences.

Get to the point quickly (similar to writing). Stop speaking before they stop listening!

Summarise in your mind what is being said. If listening to a public speaker or trainer, jot down the main ideas. This will remind you of other things said as well.

Credibility

Communicating credibility focuses on the communication skills necessary to build trust and credibility in any communication situation: formal or informal, seated or standing, face-to-face or over the phone, and in your work and personal lives.

Make sure your body language reinforces what you are saying.

Make eye contact.

Don't speak too fast. Take your time.

Be consistent with what you have said in the past.

When answering questions, don't bluff. Tell them you will 'look it up' or 'think about it' and get back to them.

You can't know everything; if you pretend you do, you will lose credibility.

Using hand gestures can help you convey your message with sincerity. This can help you emphasize points, reflect on your emotions, and paint a picture in your listeners' minds. By using gestures that come naturally to you, you will burn off energy that helps you relax. Notice what you do with your hands when in your most comfortable settings, such as with your family and friends. Try expressing naturally with your hands the next time in a business setting.

- Always know your audience and how formally or informally they behave and adjust your gestures as needed.

- Let your arms relax at your sides when you are not gesturing. Avoid elbow lock, hands in pockets, hand clasping, arms crossing, or placing your hands in any other place that is not natural. Gestures should be used when you are on the phone, too. Remember, gestures animate our voice.

Facial expressions reflect how you feel. If you feel excited about something, your face must show it. If you are discussing a frustrating topic and want to convey a sense of frustration to your listeners, your face must reveal that also. Showing some emotion is key. You don't want to smile all the time.

But if you want to convey sincerity and persuade your listeners to do something, seeing some emotion on your face will help them feel you are serious about your topic and how you feel about it. When a smile is appropriate, let it out.

Your listeners will tend to mirror your smile. With an occasional smile, you relax, and they relax, and that can turn a tense situation around.

You may find it distracting or bothersome when you are talking with someone or hear a speech that includes filler words such as 'um,' 'you know,' 'like,' or any other word spoken too frequently. Retaining much of the content can be difficult when someone speaks with too many filler words.

The pause is the cure for eliminating filler words in any communication situation. The first step is to become aware of your filler words. Once you recognize your filler word, replace it with a pause. Catch yourself not ever ending a sentence or plugging gaps with filler words, and then build in the discipline of silence.

The Discipline of Silence

Silence allows the listeners to:

- Soak in and process what you said
- Anticipate what you will say next
- Take notes
- Ask a question

Listeners need silence. They become disgruntled if they don't get it. Pausing helps your listeners stay engaged.

The benefits you get from pausing include:

- Time to breathe
- Remaining poised and in control

- Being able to emphasize a point

- Listening more effectively.

You can practice the pause in everyday situations by listening to your voicemails before re-recording the message. Hence, it is 'filler-free' or free of run-on sentences, and notice if you run out of breath or your volume trails off at the end of sentences. If it does, commit to pausing and breathing sooner and asking family, friends, and colleagues to notice your filler words in casual situations.

Importance of Eye Contact in Communication

Eye contact is extremely important in all your interactions, no matter who the listeners are or in any business or personal situation. Having good eye contact with your listener not only helps to establish your credibility but also helps you establish a better relationship with your listeners. Here are a few guidelines:

- Look people in the eye – not over their heads, at their noses, or the room's back wall.

- Look at people for a thought, phrase, or wherever there is a punctuation mark. When you see a comma, period, exclamation mark, or question mark, pause and shift your eyes to the next person.

- Be sure to make eye contact with everyone in the room. Do not ignore anyone.

- Be sure your eye contact is random; that way, it looks natural.

- During one-on-one situations, notice if the other person is uncomfortable; halt eye contact briefly, and then reconnect. When you look away, don't look over the person's shoulder; instead, use an object situated between the two of you.

Communicating with Confidence

Communicating confidently is a straightforward guide to making good conversation that works in any situation and for any personality type. If you have confidence, you will communicate more effectively.

Confidence allows you to speak concisely and with clarity. Professionals who communicate with confidence can convey their desired information to their clients and co-workers clearly and efficiently. Effective communication is critical for career advancement.

A confident communicator is grounded, comfortable in their skin, at ease, and natural, whether in a one-on-one conversation, a meeting at work, or online.

If you also struggle with communicating confidently, use the following tips to help you gain confidence:

Slow Down Your Speech

It can be very easy to default to speaking quickly when nervous. While it's important not to talk at a super slow pace (try to create a speech rhythm similar to a lyrical song), it's really important to slow down your speech for many reasons:

a. It projects a more thoughtful response.

b. It allows other people to understand what you're saying and grasp the information.

c. It makes you less nervous and fearful when public speaking.

Create A Strong, Go-To, Confident Opening Sentence

Half of the battle regarding confidence is word choice, especially initially. A strong opening creates the foundation for how people will perceive your speech. Hence, avoid starting sentences with filler words.

Create An Outline of Your Thoughts to Avoid Being Interrupted

A common problem when it comes to speaking confidently is not knowing what to do when you are interrupted. When you are interrupted, you might not know how to respond. To avoid being interrupted, create an outline of your ideas and summarise them at the beginning; then, people will be more likely to wait until you're done.

Don't Be Afraid Of Silence

Silence has a time and place. If there is silence, do not feel the need to fill the void immediately. If you are having a discussion or are in a meeting that is met with silence, let it stay silent for a while. People may be collecting their thoughts.

A part of being confident in your communication is having confidence in your thoughts and ideas. So, you don't have to rush to explain it again or clarify anything if no one has asked a question. Instead of filling the silence with more filler speech, ask a question.

Let People Ask Questions

As someone with a lot of self-doubts, I know what it's like to want to overexplain everything. But talking too much is also a sign of low confidence in communication. No one wants to read an essay-styled email or listen to a presentation for 30 minutes that could have been explained in five minutes.

You don't have to be dominating a meeting or conversation to exude confidence. Confident communication is about demonstrating knowledge of your topic and sharing your ideas without second-guessing yourself and how others understand the information.

You created a clear response to an idea, and it's up to the other person to ask for clarification if they do not understand.

Listen More Than You Speak

Lastly, if you are speaking in a meeting, listen more than you speak. Being confident in your communication is also about understanding other people's perspectives and ideas when responding to them.

If you speak non-stop and never listen to the other person, they won't perceive your communication style as knowledgeable or confident because you didn't listen to anything they said. A part of confident communication is listening.

Summary

Excellence in education stems from high-quality stakeholder relationships; communication is the key to building these relationships. Effective communication creates positive school cultures wherein staff can adapt and embrace change.

Increased skill in all components of effective communication decreases the fear associated with challenging conversations. Trust is essential to building strong relationships among stakeholders. Clarity of intent increases transparency, and active listening supports people to process feedback and implement changes for growth.

These essential characteristics build the strong stakeholder relationships necessary for productive schools focused on improvement. Communication will enable the maintenance of relationships while delivering honest assessments, challenging colleagues, engaging in difficult conversations, and creating partnerships with families.

Clear communication is essential in online teaching since it helps students understand the material and stay on track with the course. This can be achieved by using straightforward language, providing clear instructions, and using visual aids such as diagrams or images to supplement the text. Clear communication also helps students identify and ask questions about the material, leading to better engagement and learning outcomes.

Confidence is also important in online teaching since it can help establish students' trust and credibility. By demonstrating confidence in their teaching, instructors can inspire confidence in their students and create a positive learning environment. This can be achieved by being well-prepared for class, responsive to student questions, and open to feedback.

Credibility is another important aspect of online teaching because it helps to establish trust and respect with students. By demonstrating expertise in their subject matter, instructors can establish themselves as credible sources of information and inspire confidence in their students. This can be achieved by staying current with research in their field, sharing relevant industry experience, and highlighting their qualifications and certifications.

Communicating with greater clarity, confidence, and credibility is vital in online teaching because it helps establish trust and credibility with students, leading to better engagement and learning outcomes. Clear communication ensures students understand the material and stay on track, confidence helps to establish trust and credibility, and credibility establishes trust and respect with students.

Chapter 11: The Most Common Mistakes to Avoid When Teaching Online

Online teachers are lucky because they can work from home almost anywhere in the world. Still, they also encounter unique problems. Of course, some issues are similar to problems experienced in classrooms; however, online teachers will have to deal with them differently.

Some teachers are new to online teaching, but some have been doing it for years.

But, no matter what, nobody wants to look unprofessional if you're a novice or an old timer. You might think only inexperienced teachers risk looking incompetent because you tend to think they lack experience. Those who have been teaching for years may make the occasional blunder, too. So, when it comes to looking and acting like a pro, we're all in the same boat.

Here are some mistakes you'll want to avoid if you want to be taken seriously as an online teacher.

Camera and Appearance

If you use a webcam for your classes, please consider your appearance and background. Just because you work at home does not mean that you can wear your nightwear/loungewear during classes. Dressing appropriately and professionally will help earn your students' respect and set the tone for your interactions with them.

Keep in mind that students will not only see you but also everything behind you. Beds and bathrooms should not be seen in the background. Find a quiet, neutral place that reveals little personal information.

Getting to know students is great, but they should not see certain parts of your house, family members walking behind you, or pets. You must demonstrate a professional approach to your work and take their education seriously.

Microphone Placement

Microphone placement is also another essential point that teachers need to consider. Online teachers must use a headset. If you do not, students will be distracted by your typing, clicking, and other sounds, but using a headset reduces the number of different noises they hear and allows them to focus more on what you are saying.

Microphone placement is important because it will affect the sound quality of your classes. If it is directly in front of your mouth, your breathing and speaking will cause students to hear sounds you would expect to hear if a caller is outside on a windy day.

You should test your microphone placement by recording yourself speaking into it or asking a friend or family member to test it with you using a service like Skype or Google Voice. This will give you some insight as to where it should be placed. Generally, the microphone should be off to one side and a little above or below your mouth.

Overtalking

Online teachers often spend too much time speaking during lessons, primarily if they are not used to teaching one-on-one lessons. Since online classes are generally short, teachers should maximize student talking time. If you use certain teaching material, allow students to read directions and anything else you may be tempted to read for them.

Use your speaking time to ask questions, prompt longer responses, give feedback, and model pronunciation. Encourage students to ask questions. For example, instead of having a student say each word on a vocabulary list after you, have them read the words aloud, practice the pronunciation of any words they had difficulty with, and ask if there are any new words on the list.

This saves a lot of time because you only have to focus on what the student needs help with.

Lack of Variety

Online teachers focus most of their attention on speaking and listening. These are very important skills, but to learn English, students should focus on all aspects of the language, which includes reading and writing.

To make the best use of your time, you can ask students to read materials before class to prepare them for lessons and assign written work occasionally as homework. Some students may not be interested in improving their writing skills, but be sure to establish what they want to get out of their lessons so that you can plan classes appropriately.

Encourage students to consider the importance of these skills and explain how including them in lessons will not take significant time away from other activities.

Insufficient Feedback

It is important to provide students with written feedback and evaluations. It can be hard to structure this without homework assignments or tests, but students should have a record of their progress and be able to review their mistakes in their own time.

Online learners must do some self-study activities in addition to taking online classes, though without direction, it may be challenging for them to know what to focus on. Providing students with feedback will help you both identify which areas they struggle with, and you can recommend additional practical exercises to help them.

Another point to consider: it is nice to know what time of day it is for your students.

This seems very simple, but the class you teach in the morning might be in the evening for your students, so you should adjust your greeting accordingly. This can be a challenge, but it lets students know you are invested in them enough to know what time and day your class is in their country. It personalizes your experience a little more.

Not Being Prepared

This is fairly obvious and a mistake most teachers try to avoid. However, there are different levels of preparedness. You have a solid lesson plan and the right materials – but are you prepared for the unexpected?

What will you do if your internet connection fails, your laptop starts acting up, or the website you wanted to see is temporarily unavailable?

And that's just in terms of technology, where many things can go wrong.

But, suppose technology is not an issue.

Have you fully checked the materials you'll be using?

Is there anything you're unsure about, perhaps a very technical term in the reading or a grammar point you're not confident teaching?

Being prepared involves expecting the unexpected (in terms of things that could go wrong) but also anticipating students' needs and doubts.

Being Disorganized

Preparedness and organization go hand-in-hand, and there's no better way to lose credibility than being in a constant state of disorganization.

Do you know where all of your materials are?

How do you keep track of assignments or grades?

When you want to use a piece of realia, tool, or toy, can you get it within a few seconds, or do you need to search through several folders?

The problem with being disorganized is that it makes you look unprofessional and wastes precious minutes of your students' time.

Taking Things Personally

This can happen when a student drops out of the course, and you feel devastated. Or they're not motivated and don't participate in class. Now and then, a student may even confess they 'hate learning.' Do not automatically assume it's your fault.

Although there's a lot you can do to help students overcome certain learning barriers, some things are beyond your control. And their love/hate of the English language is one of them. A real pro offers to help, sets realistic goals for the student, and tries to motivate them.

Nevertheless, a real pro can't get emotional over a student who hates studying or does not want to continue learning. If you feel confident you've given your best, let it go.

Not Delivering What You Promised

If you start the school year by promising results, you'd better deliver them (and if you promise realistic results, that should not be a problem). If you say you'll start each class by establishing a learning goal, then that's what you should do.

If you tell a group of young learners that they'll get coupons for completing an activity, you'd better whip them out at the end of the lesson. Don't make any promises if you're in doubt about what you'll deliver.

However, being inconsistent, that is, saying you'll do one thing and then doing something else, or worse yet, completely forgetting, is most unprofessional.

Confessing You're a Newbie

We've all been there. We've all had a first day on the job. We've all been newbie teachers. But even if you're a newbie, there's no need to give your class full disclosure. If they ask, don't lie to them.

However, don't start a class by saying, "I'm new. In fact, this is the very first lesson I'll be teaching. Please bear with me if I make some mistakes."

In the words of the famous sports brand, 'Just Do It.' Start teaching and do the best you can. Chances are your students won't notice minor mistakes if you seem confident and act like you know what you're doing.

Underestimating Your Students

Quite often, we come across students who have more initiative than most. And on the other hand, teachers underestimate them. Messages like, "This is too hard for you," will not only squash their natural curiosity and motivation, but it will make you look bad because you're supposed to encourage them and support them in their efforts.

It does not mean that you can't give them realistic expectations. The students we most often underestimate are children. You'd be surprised at what they can understand and accomplish. So, resist the urge to make a game, exercise, or test 'easier' because 'they're just kids.' See if they're up to a challenge instead!

Forgetting Important Facts About Your Students

Needless to say, you should learn your students' names as fast as you can. Not only that, though. Getting their professions, nationalities, or personal details mixed up is not cool. You then give the impression that you're simply not interested when you should be doing the opposite: you should take the time to get to know them and their interests.

Nobody's Perfect, and Everybody Makes Mistakes

But some are costlier than others. Impressions count, and your success as an online teacher depends on how professional you appear. You can have one year or ten years of experience – yet you should always act like a pro.

Losing Your Temper

Losing your temper in any classroom or when teaching online can be disastrous. Showing strong negative emotions is one of the worst things you can do. All teachers have bad days, get irritated with students, and struggle to maintain composure at one time or another.

You do not want to lose your temper, so you shout, yell, or cry. If you feel angry, it might be a good idea to excuse or remove yourself from the situation for a few minutes.

Losing Control

One thing you will never regain if you lose it is your control. Don't let the students walk all over you, take control of your lesson, or get unruly in any way. Sometimes, students might become overly excited or obnoxiously loud during an activity, and you need to be able to bring them back down.

Students need to respect you; if you are too passive and don't have boundaries, you will lose control at some point. One great strategy that works with both kids and adults is to signal that they know they are expected to do the same thing and get quiet when they see it.

Some popular options are raising your hand, clapping if it isn't too noisy already, or waving. It has a domino effect. When you reach a few students, the rest will follow, and you will regain control.

Going Crazy with Handouts

Too many handouts are just not a good idea. Temper handouts with activities that involve students, and don't just keep them idle by doing boring rote work and trying to weed through your ten-page explanation. Use the discussion rooms, interact with students, and never rely on paper to do your job.

Getting Overly Involved

Depending on your circumstances, it can become pretty easy to become overly emotionally involved with your students. When teaching, you may learn a lot about students during the class, and you may even need to extend some help to them outside of classroom hours.

Be careful to have boundaries for yourself, and don't get too caught up in students' problems. Also, be wary of creating personal relationships. This can easily happen when teaching adults; just be sure it doesn't interfere with the classroom dynamic.

Making Fun of Students

It may seem obvious that you shouldn't ever mock or make fun of students, but sometimes, what seems to be a harmless joke or comment can wound a student's confidence and self-esteem.

It is a great talent to use humor in the classroom and show students how to laugh at themselves. Be careful that your jokes or sarcasm aren't aimed at particular students in a personally harmful way.

Being Late

It is very important to model the behavior you want from students. Being late occasionally or sometimes a few moments late is not a problem. When you are chronically late, you show the students it is also acceptable for them to be late.

Be as punctual as possible, and when you are late, be sure to apologize to students or let them know that you will be late in advance.

Self-Correction

For example, during a language class, a teacher might unintentionally say, "She have a new car," but they quickly catch the error and self-correct, stating, "I meant to say, 'She has a new car.'"

By using a small gesture or signal, the teacher helps the student recognize the error and prompts them to correct it independently. This process is known as self-correction in language studies.

Self-correction means that students independently rectify their mistakes instead of relying on the teacher for corrections. This natural process occurs in both oral and written language for first and second-language learners. Students who can self-correct enjoy several advantages over those who cannot.

Taking Up All the Talking Time

Those new to teaching often make this fundamental mistake: they take up too much of the talking time because they feel uncomfortable around silence or long pauses or because they are over-enthusiastic about sharing their knowledge.

Clearly, hogging most of the talking time is out of the question.

But how to find the right balance between student and teacher talking time?

In the context of student-centered and communicative language teaching approaches; generally, students should speak for 70% of the class time, while teachers speak for the remaining 30%. This means that, in most cases, your participation should be limited to giving instructions and explaining essential points, though, above all, to eliciting a response from students and facilitating all types of speaking activities.

Poor or Inconsistent Classroom Management

This is one of the mistakes that is often made due to a lack of experience. Classroom management is not an exact science; it's not like teaching the past simple tense.

Each group of students is different, and rules must be set as a group. The problem stems from the fact that new teachers may not have a clearly defined teaching style. Thus, they either become too strict or too lax.

Forgetting Cultural Differences

Some teachers are so focused on teaching things about the English culture they completely ignore that of their students. Some gestures teachers commonly use in the classroom, like the gesture for 'okay,' may be very rude in other cultures.

In some countries, students may be used to lecturing and may not react positively when you propose a game.

This is a mistake teachers make in foreign countries where the culture is very different from Western culture, like Arabic or Oriental cultures. Learn about your students' customs, especially greetings, and use this information to create a positive learning environment.

Summary

By avoiding common mistakes, instructors can help ensure that students are engaged and motivated to learn and achieve the desired learning outcomes. In doing so, instructors can help establish trust and credibility with their students, leading to a more positive and productive learning experience.

There are several reasons why it is important to avoid common mistakes when teaching online:

• **Reduced Engagement:** Students who cannot understand the material or are not engaged in the class may disengage from the course and not achieve the desired learning outcomes.

• **Decreased Motivation:** If students are not motivated to learn, they may not put in the effort required to succeed in the course.

• **Poor Student Performance:** If students cannot understand the material or are not engaged in the class, they may not perform as well as they could.

• **Loss Of Trust and Credibility:** If students do not trust or respect the instructor, they may not be as motivated to learn or may not take the course seriously.

• **Difficulty Creating a Sense of Community:** In an online learning environment, creating a sense of community among students can be difficult. If the instructor makes common mistakes, such as not being responsive to student questions or not providing clear instructions, it can further hinder community building.

• **Negative Impact on Student Satisfaction:** Common mistakes such as not providing clear instructions or not being responsive to student questions can lead to negative student evaluations and lower satisfaction rates, which can negatively impact the reputation of the instructor and the course.

Chapter 12: Greatest Persuasion

Distance education is a formal learning activity that occurs when students and instructors are separated by geographic distance or time. Learning is supported by communications technology such as television, videotape, computers, email, and radios.

Online learning encompasses any educational experience or environment primarily relying on the Internet for communication and presentation delivery. There are numerous potential benefits associated with investing in online learning, including increased access to education, enhanced learning quality, better preparation of students for a knowledge-based society, 'lifelong' learning opportunities, and profit-making.

Online education/learning allows students to receive education from the comfort of their own space without the need to attend in-person classes. Gone are the days when physical attendance was mandatory; today, thanks to technology, we can attend classes, and teachers can teach us from any corner of the world.

The only requirements for online learning are a high-speed internet connection, a smartphone, and access to an online teaching platform. If you have earphones or headphones, that would be even better.

What Is the Need for Online Learning?

You might be wondering about the necessity of online learning, especially when physical classes have been the norm for many years.

The answer to this question is quite straightforward. Following the emergence of the coronavirus, the lives of people all around the world underwent a significant transformation. Many countries implemented lockdowns, resulting in the closure of offices, schools, and colleges. Consequently, a critical need for online learning arose to make the most of the time during the pandemic. It's important to note that the concept of online education existed before the coronavirus, but its significance has grown substantially in the wake of the pandemic.

While the demand for online learning surged during the COVID-19 pandemic, it's essential to recognize that online learning had already been established as an effective mode of education prior to the global health crisis.

If you want to succeed in life, you must have some sort of education. Education is the key that opens the path to success. There was a time when getting an education was a tough task, yet today, the concept has changed; today, anyone who wants to be educated has many options to get an education.

Even the governments of many countries provide free education to many students. However, in the last few years, due to the coronavirus, the concept of traditional education has changed so much. Today, many students can attend classes online, and teachers also teach their students from their comfort zone. This all is possible due to online education.

Advantages of Online Learning

It seems everything is moving online these days, including our education. There are many advantages of online learning, and we can also get answers to the need for online education through the advantages of online learning.

Very Convenient

Over the past years, in-person learning has been the dominant approach to education. Previously, online learning options were non-existent, and everyone had to attend classes physically. However, in today's era, the availability of online learning has revolutionized education, allowing students to attend classes from the comfort of their homes.

This convenience has proven to be highly beneficial, particularly for students from small villages who previously had to bear the expense of traveling to bigger cities for their studies.

More Affordable

Moreover, pursuing an online education is generally more affordable than traditional methods. According to the Open Education Database, while not all online degrees offer lower net tuition prices, associated expenses are consistently lower. Commuting costs are eliminated, and sometimes required course materials, such as textbooks, are available online for free.

For those from low-income families, this financial burden was often impossible. Thankfully, online classes have eliminated the need to relocate, as students can now access education anywhere in the world, resulting in significant savings on food, housing, and transportation costs.

College Recognized Credits

Additionally, colleges and universities now recognize credits earned through free massive open online courses (MOOCs), further contributing to the cost-effectiveness of online education. These factors combine to make online learning a more economical choice compared to traditional offline classes or learning methods.

Accessibility to International Experts

Online learning offers the advantage of accessing training or classes from the finest teachers worldwide. The potential for global markets also opens doors for international partnerships, enriching the learning experience through diverse fellow students and access to international experts.

Unlike offline classes, where one is limited to local teachers, online classes allow students to select instructors according to their preferences, with many popular teachers providing free lessons on platforms like YouTube. This flexibility allows students to receive training from the world's best educators, all from the comfort of their homes, at no cost.

Saves Significant Time

In addition to the flexibility and international exposure, online learning saves significant time compared to offline classes. Traveling to physical classrooms and back can consume substantial periods, which becomes a crucial factor in a student's schedule.

Online classes eliminate the need for commuting, allowing students to access courses from anywhere in the world without leaving their homes. This time-saving aspect of online learning gives students more opportunities to utilize their time for other activities and interests.

Freedom to Choose

Another advantage of online education lies in the freedom to choose one's educational path. Creative individuals or those seeking specialized focus can find their dream courses without the need to relocate or compete in a highly competitive learning environment.

The wide range of online courses and majors offered by traditional universities means students can pursue their desired education without making unnecessary compromises.

Comfort of Students

Comfort is also a significant consideration for students choosing online education. Students can avoid the time and stress associated with commuting to physical institutions by attending classes remotely.

This convenience extends to situations where adverse weather conditions might hinder regular attendance. Online students can actively participate in discussions, submit assignments, and engage with course materials without the constraints of physical class sessions, granting them the flexibility to navigate their learning journey more smoothly than traditional students.

Better Demand in the Market

Moreover, employers increasingly value online courses, as they see them as a display of initiative and resourcefulness. The growing technological advancements have made online education a prevalent choice for many employees seeking to enhance their skills and knowledge. Hiring managers respect online degrees as much as those obtained from traditional brick-and-mortar institutions.

Listing relevant online courses and programs on one's resume showcases a commitment to continuous learning and professional development, which is highly appreciated in the job market. Online education is viewed as equivalent to regular education by employers and as a means of acquiring competence in the latest technologies and trends.

Set Their Own Pace

A major advantage of online education lies in its flexibility, allowing learners to study at their preferred pace. The asynchronous nature of online learning permits access to materials at any suitable time, making it convenient for individuals with work or family commitments during the day. It also enables learners to seek outside assistance without the pressure of strict deadlines. Those who wish to take more time to complete a degree can do so without feeling rushed.

Increased Participation

The online delivery method provides the added benefit of increased participation from all students, including those who may be more reserved in a physical classroom setting. The anonymity associated with online learning fosters a level playing field where instructors can treat all students equally.

Learner identity becomes important in online learning environments, with students sometimes using pseudonyms in role-plays or discussion forums. This allows learners to redefine their identities to best suit their learning preferences.

As a result of these advantages, online education is gaining popularity over traditional instruction. Students appreciate the freedom to choose their desired subjects, the comfort of learning from home, and the ability to manage their learning pace.

Online courses also carry weight on resumes, making them a well-rounded and appealing option for many individuals seeking to advance their education and career prospects. Given its numerous benefits, it is no surprise that online education is becoming increasingly prevalent in today's educational landscape.

Although online learning offers numerous advantages, such as flexibility and accessibility, it also has disadvantages. Some of the key disadvantages of online learning include:

- **Lack of Face-to-Face Interaction:** Online learning often lacks in-person interaction between students and instructors. This can lead to a sense of isolation and reduced opportunities for real-time discussions and feedback.

- **Self-Motivation and Discipline:** Online learners need to be highly self-motivated and disciplined to manage their time effectively and stay on track with coursework. Procrastination can be a significant challenge.

- **Limited Social Interaction:** Traditional classrooms provide a social environment where students can interact with peers, form study groups, and build social skills. Online learners may miss out on these social aspects of education.

- **Technical Issues:** Technical problems, such as internet connectivity issues or software glitches, can disrupt the learning experience and cause frustration for both students and instructors.

- **Quality of Instruction:** The quality of online courses can vary widely. Some may lack the rigor and engagement found in traditional classrooms, and the effectiveness of online teaching methods can vary based on the instructor's skill and the course design.

- **Dependence on Technology:** Online learning relies heavily on technology. Students who don't have access to reliable devices or the internet may be at a disadvantage.

- **Cheating and Academic Integrity:** Online exams and assessments can be vulnerable to cheating, and maintaining academic integrity can be more challenging in a remote learning environment.

- **Teacher-Student Relationships:** Building strong teacher-student relationships can be more challenging in online settings, impacting personalized support and mentorship.

- **Screen Time and Health Concerns:** Excessive screen time can lead to eye strain, fatigue, and other health issues. Online learners may need to be mindful of their screen time and take breaks to reduce these risks.

- **Limited Networking Opportunities:** Online learners may have fewer opportunities for networking and building professional connections than students who attend traditional in-person classes.

It's important to note that the extent to which these disadvantages affect a learner can vary based on individual preferences, the quality of the online course, and the support systems in place. Many of these challenges can be mitigated with proper planning, effective course design, and the development of strong online learning skills.

Benefits for Rural Areas

Online teaching has emerged as a crucial educational lifeline for students residing in remote or rural areas, addressing several challenges and enhancing their learning experiences. Here's why online teaching is of paramount importance for this demographic:

- **Overcoming Geographical Barriers:** Traditional education often falls short in remote and rural areas due to the limited availability of schools, colleges, or qualified educators. Online teaching transcends these geographical barriers, providing access to quality education regardless of location. Students in remote areas can now access a wide array of courses, from basic subjects to advanced disciplines, without the need to relocate.

- **Access to Expert Instructors:** Online teaching brings expert instructors within reach. Students in remote areas can benefit from the knowledge and guidance of skilled educators who may not be available locally. This access to experienced teachers significantly enhances the quality of education and broadens students' horizons.

- **Flexible Learning Schedules:** Online teaching offers flexible learning schedules, which are particularly valuable in rural and remote regions. Many students in these areas may have agricultural or family responsibilities that make traditional classroom attendance challenging. With online education, they can balance their daily commitments with learning, improving their chances of academic success.

- **Economic Affordability:** Pursuing education away from home often entails substantial costs, including accommodation, transportation, and other related expenses. Online teaching significantly reduces these financial burdens. Students can save on travel and accommodation costs, making education more economically viable for them and their families.

- **Overcoming Infrastructure Limitations:** Remote areas may lack adequate educational infrastructure, including libraries and well-equipped classrooms. Online teaching overcomes these limitations by providing digital access to extensive learning resources, e-libraries, and interactive content. Students can leverage these resources to supplement their education effectively.

- **Community Development:** Beyond individual benefits, online teaching can foster community development. As students in rural areas gain access to quality education, they acquire knowledge and skills that can contribute to their communities' economic and social development. This can lead to a more knowledgeable and skilled workforce, positively impacting local industries and services.

• **Diverse Educational Offerings:** Online teaching offers various courses, including vocational and technical training, empowering students to explore their interests and career prospects more comprehensively. This diversity ensures that students in rural areas are not limited by their geographic location but have access to educational opportunities.

• **Lifelong Learning Opportunities:** For adults in rural areas seeking to further their education or acquire new skills, online teaching offers a flexible pathway for lifelong learning. This is particularly important for staying competitive in the job market and adapting to evolving industries.

• **Inclusivity for Women and Girls:** Online learning benefits married women and girls from rural areas who may face limitations in pursuing education due to cultural restrictions. With online education, they can fulfill their dreams of studying and receiving an education without leaving their homes or facing societal barriers. This inclusivity empowers them to access knowledge and skills that were once out of reach.

Overall, online teaching is a transformative force that brings education to the doorsteps of students in remote and rural areas. It breaks down geographical barriers, offers access to expert instructors, accommodates flexible schedules, reduces costs, overcomes infrastructure limitations, and fosters community development. Through online education, students in these areas can unlock their full potential and contribute to the growth and development of their regions.

Summary

The entire education system has changed due to technology. Today, we don't need to leave home to attend classes. All of this is made possible because of online learning. There are several advantages to online learning.

For example, during COVID-19, when all educational institutions were closed, students were instructed online to continue their studies. Without this method, every student's education would have reached a standstill. In the coming year, online learning will dominate the education market.

Online learning has revolutionized the education system by providing greater flexibility, access, and convenience for both students and teachers. With online learning, students can attend class from anywhere and at any time, which can be especially beneficial for those with busy schedules or who live in remote areas. This flexibility also means that students can learn at their own pace, which can be more effective for some learners.

It has also increased access to education by making it more affordable and accessible to a broader range of students. Traditional in-person classes require physical classrooms and other expenses, which can be prohibitively expensive for some students. Online learning eliminates many of these costs, making education more affordable and accessible to more people.

Online learning is also more convenient for both teachers and students. It eliminates the need for commuting and allows easy access to course materials and resources, making it particularly beneficial for students living in remote areas or having mobility issues.

Moreover, it has provided a variety of options for teaching, such as videos, interactive quizzes, and live webinars, which can create a more engaging and interactive learning experience for students. This variety can also provide a more personalized experience for students, allowing teachers to adapt to different learning styles.

The recent pandemic has highlighted the importance of online learning. During the COVID-19 pandemic, when all educational institutions were closed, students were instructed online to continue their studies.

This has shown that online learning can be a reliable and effective way to continue education during unexpected events. In the coming years, online learning will continue to dominate the education market as it has proven to be a reliable and effective way to continue education during unexpected events.

The following are key advantages of effective online teaching:

- **Increased Flexibility:** Online teaching allows students to learn at their own pace and on their own schedule, which can be particularly beneficial for those with busy schedules or who live in remote areas.

- **Greater Access to Education:** Online teaching can make education more accessible to a wider range of students, including those who may not have been able to attend traditional in-person classes.

- **Cost-Effectiveness:** Online teaching can be more cost-effective than traditional in-person teaching, eliminating the need for physical classrooms and other expenses.

- **Convenience:** Online teaching can be more convenient for teachers and students, as it eliminates commuting and allows easy access to course materials and resources.

- **Variety of Teaching Options:** Online teaching provides a variety of options for teaching, such as videos, interactive quizzes, and live webinars, which can create a more engaging and interactive learning experience for students.

- **Improved Student Engagement:** Online teaching can improve student engagement by providing opportunities for interaction and collaboration, such as online discussions and group projects.

- **Better Tracking of Student Progress:** Online teaching platforms often provide tools for tracking student progress, such as quizzes, assignments, and assessments, which can help teachers identify areas where students need additional support.

- **Greater scalability:** Online teaching can be scaled up more easily than in-person teaching, allowing institutions to reach more students with the same resources.

Online learning, while offering flexibility and accessibility, has drawbacks, including limited face-to-face interaction, the need for self-motivation, reduced social interaction, technical issues, varying instruction quality, technology dependence, academic integrity concerns, teacher-student relationship challenges, screen time issues, and limited networking opportunities. The impact of these disadvantages varies based on individual factors and course quality but can be addressed with planning, effective design, and improved online learning skills.

Chapter 13: Security Concerns to Consider for Your Paid Online Courses

A successful paid online course offers unique expertise, a structured learning experience, exclusive materials, personalized support, credible certification, convenience, motivation, continuous updates, and a promising return on investment.

These factors create a compelling value proposition that attracts learners and ensures a positive and rewarding learning experience. The popularity of e-payment systems has surged due to the widespread adoption of internet-based shopping, banking, and transactions. Both individuals and businesses are increasingly opting for e-commerce.

Understanding e-Payment Systems

Throughout history, payment systems have evolved from simple barter systems to complex electronic methods. Traditional means of payment like cash, cheques, and cards have now been complemented and, in some cases, replaced by electronic payment options.

E-payments encompass various electronic transactions, including online banking, mobile-based payments, and digital wallets.

The advent of technology has also expanded the range of devices and processes used in electronic transactions, leading to a decline in cash and cheque-based transactions.

Different Types of e-Payment Systems

Various types of e-payment systems have been developed, each catering to specific needs and preferences.

Smart Card: The smart card-based system employs a plastic card with an integrated circuit chip, offering versatility and data portability. It combines multiple identification functions into one card, granting access to multiple services and networks. It employs a three-factor authentication mechanism to enhance security, incorporating Personal Identification Numbers (PINs), digital signatures, and fingerprint biometrics.

Card Payments: Credit, debit, and prepaid cards are prevalent e-payments used for various online transactions. Online payment systems are built on internet banking platforms, enabling customers to make purchases or transfer money online through secure websites operated by financial institutions.

Mobile-Based Payments: Mobile-based payment systems leverage mobile devices to enable consumers to conduct transactions via SMS, PIN, or other mobile functionalities. More sophisticated methods like NFC and infrared are expected to enhance mobile-based transactions as technology advances.

E-Wallets: The electronic wallet (e-wallet) system consolidates various functionalities into a single smart card, eliminating the need for carrying multiple cards. E-wallets offer enhanced security features and convenience for making payments and money transfers. Popular examples include PayPal, Windows Phone Wallet, and Google Wallet.

Security Threats to Consider

However, security threats have also evolved with advancements in e-payment systems. Viruses, worms, Trojan horses, and Denial of Service (DoS) attacks pose significant risks to e-payment security. Attackers exploit vulnerabilities in computer systems or trick users into revealing sensitive information. Robust security measures, such as encryption, multi-factor authentication, and continuous monitoring, are crucial to mitigate these threats.

With this rise in e-payment usage, there has also been a significant increase in malicious activities targeting online banking, leading to unauthorized access, theft, and fraud.

Various threats like worms, Trojans, viruses, phishing, and other cybercrimes have emerged, necessitating robust information security measures for effective e-payment systems. In response to this growing concern, some countries have enacted specific legislation to protect e-payment systems and combat cybercrime.

Common Attacks Used by Cybercriminals

Cybercriminals use phishing and pharming tactics to deceive individuals and obtain their personal information by impersonating trustworthy entities. Both techniques have been employed for online identity theft, where sensitive information is stolen.

Phishing

Phishing attacks typically involve sending fraudulent emails or creating malicious websites that appear legitimate, requesting users to provide account information under the pretext of addressing an issue. Once the attackers receive the requested data, they can gain unauthorized access to the victim's accounts.

Pharming

Pharming, conversely, involves redirecting a user's internet connection to a fake website, even when the correct address is entered into the browser. This can be achieved by altering the host file on the victim's computer or exploiting vulnerabilities in the DNS server software.

Man-In-The-Middle Attack

Advancements in e-payment systems have introduced new aggressive and intrusive attack methods. One such method is the Man-In-The-Middle attack, where attackers intercept and modify exchanged data during an ongoing connection. These attacks can be combined with spamming or email bombing, where hackers inundate a computer or network with thousands of unsolicited emails.

Drive-by Downloads

Drive-by downloads represent another significant threat to e-payment security. Users unknowingly download malware when visiting seemingly legitimate websites contaminated with harmful codes.

Masquerading

Masquerading, also known as spoofing, involves impersonating someone else by falsifying data, often achieved by sending messages that appear to be from a different source. These tactics pose serious risks to the security and privacy of online payment transactions.

Summary

This chapter delves into the security aspects of paid online courses, emphasizing the value proposition they offer. E-payment systems have witnessed substantial growth due to the prevalence of internet-based transactions. The evolution of payment methods from cash to electronic systems is explored, including smart cards, card payments, mobile-based payments, and e-wallets.

However, alongside these advancements come security threats. Viruses, worms, Trojan horses, and Denial of Service (DoS) attacks pose significant risks to e-payment security. Unauthorized access, theft, and fraud have surged in online banking. The chapter also highlights common cyberattacks such as phishing, pharming, Man-In-The-Middle attacks, drive-by downloads, and masquerading.

Robust security measures like encryption, multi-factor authentication, and continuous monitoring are vital to mitigate these threats. The chapter underscores the importance of information security to ensure the safety and privacy of online payment transactions.

Chapter 14: How to Sell Your Online Course

Entrepreneurs come in all types, creating what's innovative and selling the unexpected. This description certainly applies to online course creators, a category of entrepreneurs selling their knowledge and expertise. Online course creators package their insights—knowledge, know-how, and experience—into a digital bundle for customers without worrying about packing tape, shipping labels, and tracking numbers.

There's a good chance you have specialized knowledge or expertise that others can learn from. You might know how to edit and produce videos, have unique insights on growing social media channels, or be uniquely skilled in digital design.

Creating an online course is about taking your knowledge and skills – often honed over years or even decades – and developing a curriculum to compress and share your expertise with others so they can learn, too.

With just a laptop and access to the internet, your online course can enroll students worldwide, helping them master important skills at a much lower cost than traditional education.

There's never been a better time to sell digital products like a course and be part of a movement and industry democratizing education.

The Benefits of Creating an Online Course

With no inventory issues or supply chain problems to solve, creating a digital course is an online business idea with various benefits worth considering, including:

• **Online Courses Are Scalable** – Creating an online course takes a lot of time and effort. However, with digital products, you can create a single resource and sell it to hundreds, thousands, or even millions of people around the world. This process can be entirely automated so that anyone can buy your course with a few clicks. With digital products, you're not limited by the constraints of selling physical goods, like product inventory and packaging costs.

• **Online Courses Are Low-Cost** – It's often inexpensive to create a course. Depending on the type of course you create, you may just need a few software subscriptions to host your course, send emails to prospective buyers, and build a community of learners. While creating a full-fledged video course can be more expensive, you can cut costs by opting for an inexpensive camera, using basic lighting and a mid-range microphone to start – aim to make your video course look 'professional,' not necessarily 'high-budget production.' Aside from production costs, marketing can also be manageable.

- **Online Courses Have High Margins** - After the costs that go into production and marketing, the remaining revenue from a course can be profit. While many traditional entrepreneurs selling physical products have slim margins, digital products like courses can have margins as high as 85% – for instance, selling a course for £100 and keeping £85.

- **Online Courses Generate Passive Income** - While passive income is never truly passive—there's upfront time, money, and effort—online courses come close. Once you've created the course, you can generate income from it continuously. This is especially true if your course is download-only and not a cohort-based course with a live or community component.

If you are convinced of the benefits of creating an online course, dive into the step-by-step process of taking your course from a little idea to launch day and beyond.

Understanding Your Unique Selling Point

The rise of e-learning and the benefits of creating an online course should signal something important: you'll have competition when bringing your online course to the market. There is no shortage of online courses on topics ranging from digital marketing and video editing to online writing and entrepreneurship.

When considering creating an online course, choose a topic you're *uniquely suited* to teach. Select a course topic where you have industry insight, credibility, expertise, and passion. Plus, ensure the course topic has high market demand.

Industry Expertise

Consideration of industry insight, expertise, and credibility is essential when developing an online course. Learners prefer to learn from experts with extensive experience in the subject matter and are respected within their field.

Signs that you possess these qualities include:

- Years of industry experience
- A deep knowledge of the course subject acquired over time, historical context in the industry
- The ability to make informed predictions about the industry's future
- Above-average skills in the subject matter
- And the ability to mentor and guide novices
- As well as having credentials and accolades that highlight your expertise

A Thought Leader

Being recognized as a thought leader in your area and regularly sharing your knowledge with a substantial audience through platforms like social media, podcasts, and articles also indicates your credibility and expertise.

Your Passion

Furthermore, passion plays a crucial role in creating a compelling course. It requires a meaningful investment of time and energy, and signs of your passion include genuine enthusiasm for your subject area and the ability to transmit that excitement to your students.

Desire to Help

A desire to help people acquire skills and knowledge in your field, a willingness to go above and beyond to offer a superior course compared to competitors, and being thrilled about organizing a curriculum around your expertise is also indicative of your passion.

Continuous Improvement

Additionally, continuously striving for improvement and mastery in your field showcases your dedication and passion for what you are doing.

Figuring Out Your Market Demand

However, while expertise and passion are vital, ensuring sufficient market demand for your course to succeed is equally important. Factors indicating high market interest in your course include being in a growing industry, having a high search volume on platforms like Google, having competitors offering similar courses, teaching a skill set that is in high demand, and identifying an underserved audience in your niche that you can cater to.

Customer Research

Conducting thorough customer research is crucial before creating an online course. Understanding your target audience allows you to tailor your course content and marketing strategies to address their needs effectively. Through user research, you can put yourself in the shoes of a beginner, identify customer pain points, learn about their goals, and develop precise messaging that resonates with your ideal customers.

Using Tools for Trends

Tools like Google Trends and Ubersuggest can provide insights into search trends and audience demographics. At the same time, platforms like Reddit, Quora, and social media can help you discover relevant conversations and challenges prospective buyers face. Phone interviews with potential customers can also offer valuable direct feedback and insights.

Considering these aspects, the format and delivery of your course become significant considerations. Your course structure will impact how you market, price, and package your content and how it resonates with your target audience and provides value to your students.

Main Types of Courses to Consider

There are three main types of courses: mini-courses, multi-day courses, and masterclasses.

Mini-Course

A mini-course is relatively short and can be completed within an hour or two. It may be delivered through different mediums, such as a series of emails or a playlist of short videos. Mini-courses are often offered at a low price or even for free as a marketing tool to attract students to more comprehensive and paid course offerings. They are an excellent way for course creators to start and test the market before developing larger courses.

Multi-Day Course

Multi-day courses are intermediate-level digital educational products that take several days for students to complete. They typically include prerecorded videos organized into different modules and supplementary materials like worksheets and checklists. These courses fall into a mid-range price point. Multi-day courses are ideal if you have already validated your course idea through a mini-course.

Masterclass

Masterclasses are comprehensive courses that span several weeks or even months. They are designed to provide buyers with a complete system for success. Masterclasses are generally targeted at professionals and command higher prices. As a course creator, it is advisable not to start with a masterclass as your first course. Instead, build your experience by creating mini-courses and multi-day courses.

Choose the type of course based on your experience, the depth and breadth of the content, and your target audience's willingness to pay.

Additionally, when creating course content, determine the course formats of your lessons based on the type of course you're offering. Simple formats like emails and short videos may suffice for mini-courses, while more intensive and higher-priced courses benefit from a mix of formats to keep students engaged. Formats such as video content, screencasts, text content, downloadable content, and workbooks can be employed effectively.

Validating Marketing Demand

Validating marketing demand means that you have to pick a mode of marketing that will enhance the value of your course in the eyes of your target audience.

The following are some ways that you can do that:

Webinars

Consider creating a webinar with an upsell to validate the market demand for your course idea. This allows you to test your topic, receive feedback to refine your value proposition, prototype your course content in a condensed format, and gain insights about your audience.

The average conversion rate of a webinar can be around 20%, which can indicate market demand for your larger course. Collect participant feedback during the webinar to understand what they found valuable and their preferences. Frame future marketing efforts based on the characteristics of those who converted.

Pre-Selling

Another approach is pre-selling the course, which means selling the course before it's fully created. This strategy helps you avoid creating a course that might not find an audience. Additionally, it stress-tests your concept, allows you to tailor content based on early feedback, and raises funds through pre-sales to finance course development. Having early sign-ups can serve as motivation to complete and launch the course.

Email Marketing

Prioritize email marketing to capture the emails of prospective buyers and keep them informed about updates, information, and discounts related to your course. Utilize appearances on podcasts to establish authority and demonstrate expertise through conversations. Social media marketing, running paid ads, and implementing a content marketing strategy are other valuable marketing channels to explore.

Feedback and Testimonials

Collect feedback and testimonials from satisfied customers to showcase the value of your course and its results. Use feedback to continuously improve the course and enhance the learning experience for your students.

Figuring Out Your Pain Points

Before embarking on the sales cycle, focus on understanding your students' pain points, identifying what your ideal students want to achieve, and knowing how to sell your course to them effectively. Personalizing your teaching approach, highlighting the benefits of the course, and using social proof are essential elements of successful course promotion.

By understanding your ideal students, highlighting the benefits of the course, and using various marketing channels, you can effectively sell, attract, and retain students who are interested in the course.

Pricing For Profitability

Setting the right price for your online course is crucial to ensure profitability. This involves considering various factors that contribute to the overall cost of the course and determining a price that not only covers these costs but also generates a profit. Several key elements should be taken into account during the pricing process:

- **Cost of goods:** Assess the costs of producing the course, such as materials, equipment, and software. Additionally, consider the costs associated with hosting the course, such as rent, utilities, and internet charges.

- **Labor costs:** Factor in the time and effort spent creating and delivering the course. If you hire instructors or staff, include their expenses as well.

- **Competitive pricing:** Research the prices of similar courses in your industry to ensure your course is competitively priced.

- **Target market:** Understand your target audience's budget and willingness to pay for your course. Tailor the price to align with their expectations.

- **Revenue goals:** Set specific revenue goals for your course and price it accordingly to meet those objectives.

- **Time frame:** Consider the duration of the course; longer courses can typically be priced higher than shorter ones.

- **Quality of the course:** Evaluate the level of expertise, the course's overall quality, and the added value it offers to determine the appropriate pricing.

- **Discounts and promotions:** Offer discounts or promotions strategically to attract students and generate revenue.

Remember that pricing is not a one-time decision; it requires regular reviews and adjustments based on market conditions, competition, and revenue goals. Be flexible and open to modifying your pricing strategy to ensure long-term profitability.

Smart Marketing

Smart marketing is the strategic use of marketing efforts to reach and engage with your target audience effectively. To implement smart marketing for your online course, consider the following essential components:

• **Understand your target audience:** Conduct thorough research to gain insights into your target audience's demographics, interests, and behaviors. This knowledge will help you create personalized marketing messages that resonate with them.

• **Define your unique selling proposition (USP):** Identify what makes your course stand out from others and use it to create a compelling USP that communicates your course's distinct value.

• **Utilize multiple channels:** Diversify your marketing efforts by leveraging various channels such as social media, email marketing, content marketing, and paid advertising. Each channel serves a unique purpose in reaching your audience.

• **Create compelling content:** Develop high-quality, engaging content that showcases the value of your course and illustrates how it benefits your target audience.

• **Use data and analytics:** Make data-driven decisions by using data and analytics to track the effectiveness of your marketing efforts. Analyzing this data helps you refine your marketing strategy for optimal results.

- **Test and iterate:** Experiment with different marketing strategies and tactics and continually iterate based on what works best for your specific audience.

- **Collaborate and network:** Establish partnerships with other educators, influencers, and industry experts to expand your reach and build credibility within your niche.

- **Continuously engage:** Communicate constantly with your audience to build trust, loyalty, and excitement about your course. Keep them informed about new developments and offerings.

Selling on an Online Learning Platform

Selling your courses on an established online learning platform offers a great opportunity to access a larger audience and generate revenue. Implementing effective strategies will increase your course's visibility and appeal to potential students.

Here are some strategies for successful course sales on an online learning platform:

- **Choose the right platform:** Research various online learning platforms to find the one that aligns best with your course content and target audience.

Select a platform with a strong user base and features that cater to your course needs.

- **Optimize your course listing:** Create an appealing course listing with high-quality images, clear and concise language, and persuasive copy that highlights the value and benefits of your course.

- **Promote your course:** Leverage social media, email marketing, and other marketing channels to promote and drive traffic to your course listing. Engage with potential students and answer their queries promptly.

- **Use affiliate marketing:** Collaborate with influencers, bloggers, or other educators to promote your course. Offering an affiliate program incentivizes others to market your course and earn commissions for each successful referral.

- **Offer discounts and promotions:** Attract potential students by periodically offering discounts or limited-time promotions. This encourages them to take action and enroll in your course.

- **Optimize for search:** Utilize search engine optimization (SEO) techniques in your course listing, such as incorporating relevant keywords and meta tags to improve your visibility in search results.

- **Create a landing page:** Develop a dedicated landing page for your course designed to convert visitors into students. Use persuasive copy and clear calls to action to encourage sign-ups.

• **Utilize analytics:** Monitor and analyze performance metrics of your course listing and marketing efforts. Utilize data insights to make informed decisions and continuously improve your course's performance.

Creating a Sales Funnel

Developing a sales funnel for your online course involves guiding potential students through a series of stages that lead to their enrolment. A well-designed sales funnel can effectively convert leads into paying students.

Here are the key components of a successful sales funnel:

• **Awareness:** Raise awareness about your course and brand through a well-designed website, social media presence, and content marketing efforts that reach your target audience.

• **Interest:** Capture the interest of potential students by providing them with valuable free resources, such as webinars, e-books, or sample classes, that showcase the benefits of your course.

• **Desire:** Build desire for your course by highlighting its unique selling points and demonstrating how it can help students achieve their goals and address their pain points.

•	**Action:** Encourage potential students to take action by providing a clear call-to-action and making the enrolment process seamless and user-friendly.

•	**Follow-up:** After students enroll in your course, implement a follow-up strategy to engage with them and provide additional resources and support. This enhances their learning experience and builds brand loyalty.

•	**Optimize:** Continuously optimize your sales funnel by testing different strategies, analyzing data, and making data-driven decisions to improve conversion rates and overall performance.

A well-structured sales funnel allows you to nurture leads, build relationships, and ultimately convert them into loyal and satisfied students. By implementing these strategies, you can effectively market and sell your online course to a broader audience while achieving your revenue goals.

Tips to Create a Successful Sales Funnel

To create a successful sales funnel for your online course, you must comprehensively understand your target audience and employ effective marketing strategies. A compelling call to action is essential to drive conversions and generate revenue.

Follow these steps to build a sales funnel that maximizes the potential of your online course:

• **Define Your Target Audience:** Conduct comprehensive market research to identify your ideal students. Create detailed buyer personas, including demographics, interests, pain points, goals, and motivations. Understanding your target audience allows you to tailor your marketing messages and course content to meet their needs.

• **Optimize Your Landing Page:** Your course landing page is your online storefront and needs to make a strong impression. Design it with a clean and visually appealing layout. Clearly showcase your course's unique features, benefits, and learning outcomes. Use persuasive language and compelling visuals to communicate the value of your course to potential customers.

• **Leverage Social Media:** Utilize various social media platforms to reach and engage with your target audience. Share valuable content related to your course regularly, such as tips, snippets, and success stories. Participate in relevant discussions and groups to establish yourself as an authority in your niche. Consider using paid social media advertising to expand your reach and attract potential students.

• **Offer Free Content:** Create high-quality free content that provides value to your target audience.

This could be in the form of blog posts, video tutorials, webinars, or downloadable resources. Use these free resources to showcase your expertise and build trust with your audience. Include calls to action in the content to direct interested individuals to your course landing page.

• **Use Email Marketing:** Build an email list by offering valuable lead magnets such as free e-books, cheat sheets, or mini-courses in exchange for email addresses. Use email marketing to nurture leads, provide valuable insights, and promote your course with well-crafted email campaigns. Personalize your emails based on the interests and behaviors of your subscribers.

• **Partner with Influencers:** Identify influencers, bloggers, or industry experts with a significant following in your niche. Collaborate with them to promote your course to their audience. Offer them an affiliate commission or free enrolment. Influencer endorsements can bring targeted traffic and credibility to your course.

• **Use Referral Marketing:** Encourage your existing students to refer their friends, family, or colleagues to your course. Offer incentives such as discounts, cash rewards, or exclusive bonuses for successful referrals. Referral marketing can help you acquire new customers at a lower cost and boost your course sales.

- **Provide Social Proof:** Showcase testimonials, case studies, and success stories from satisfied students who have benefited from your course. Display these on your website, landing page, and marketing materials to build trust and credibility with potential customers. Social proof reassures prospects that your course delivers real value and results.

- **Create a Sense of Urgency:** Use scarcity and time-limited offers to create a sense of urgency among potential customers. Offer limited-time discounts, early bird pricing, or exclusive bonuses to encourage immediate enrolment. Communicate the benefits of taking action quickly to avoid missing out on the opportunity.

- **Offer a Money-Back Guarantee:** Reduce the risk for potential customers by offering a no-questions-asked money-back guarantee. This demonstrates your confidence in the quality of your course and provides reassurance to hesitant buyers. A money-back guarantee can boost conversions and give students peace of mind.

- **Offer a FREE Consultation Session:** Provide potential customers the opportunity to book a FREE Consultation Session with you or your team. This session focuses on understanding their needs, challenges, and goals. Tailor your course recommendations and address their specific concerns. This personalized approach builds trust and helps potential students see the value of your course.

- **Create an Intake Form:** Before offering a FREE Consultation Session, use an intake form to gather relevant information about potential customers. This form helps you qualify leads and identify the right clients to focus on. Understanding their background and goals ensures that you spend time with qualified leads who are more likely to enroll in your course.

- **Follow-up with the Revolvers:** After conducting the FREE Consultation Session or a free webinar, follow up with leads who may not have been qualified or didn't finish the session. Re-engage them with relevant offers or information to rekindle their interest and encourage enrolment.

- **Provide Excellent Client Support:** Offer exceptional customer support to your students throughout their learning journey. Respond promptly to their questions and concerns, and provide them with the help they need to succeed in your course. Positive experiences lead to satisfied customers more likely to recommend your course to others.

- **Continuously Improve Your Course:** Regularly gather student feedback to identify areas of improvement in your course. Use this feedback to make necessary updates and enhancements to enhance the learning experience. Continuously adding value to your course keeps it relevant and attractive to both new and returning students.

By implementing this 'Ready-To-Go' selling strategy, you can optimize your online course sales, reach your target audience effectively, and generate revenue more efficiently.

Summary

Creating an online course allows entrepreneurs to convert their expertise, knowledge, and skills into a valuable product with a global reach. Packaging their insights into a digital format allows them to deliver the course to students while minimizing overhead costs efficiently. Once established, the course can be sold to unlimited students, allowing for passive income over time.

Online courses also allow entrepreneurs to work from anywhere and on their own schedule, empowering them to take control of their careers and tailor their businesses to suit their lifestyles. Embracing the power of a well-designed sales funnel and a robust marketing strategy can help entrepreneurs succeed in the competitive online education market, stand out among competitors, and achieve long-term growth and success.

Online courses can democratize education by breaking down barriers to access and affordability.

They provide a more inclusive learning environment, offering knowledge and skills to a wider range of people who may not have had the opportunity to attend traditional in-person classes due to geographical constraints or financial limitations.

Developing and selling online courses allows teachers to position themselves as experts in their respective fields. By sharing their expertise in a structured and comprehensive manner, they can build trust and credibility among their audience, attracting new clients, customers, or opportunities for career growth.

Creating an online course can be a deeply fulfilling experience for course creators. They get to share their knowledge and insights, helping learners improve their abilities and achieve their goals. Witnessing the positive impact on students' lives can be incredibly rewarding.

One of the major advantages of online courses is their scalability. Once a course is created, it can be sold to unlimited students without additional effort or resources. This allows course creators to earn a passive income over time and reach a vast audience.

Online courses have significantly lower overhead costs compared to traditional brick-and-mortar businesses. There's no need for physical classrooms or printing materials, reducing upfront investment and ongoing expenses.

Online course creators benefit from unparalleled flexibility, allowing them to design, create, and manage their courses from any location and at any time, according to their own schedule. The power of the internet grants these courses global reach, attracting students from all corners of the world and providing a broader customer base, thus expanding the potential for course sales.

By packaging their knowledge into digital products, course creators can unlock increased earning potential compared to traditional teaching or consulting methods, as successful online courses can generate substantial revenue streams. This monetization of expertise enables entrepreneurs to leverage their accumulated knowledge and experience, transforming it into a valuable educational resource.

Moreover, online course creators can utilize advanced tracking and measurement tools to monitor student engagement, progress, and success rates, leading to improved course content and teaching methods that foster better learning outcomes. The subscription-based model of online courses presents a recurring revenue potential, providing course creators with stability and predictability in their income streams.

Beyond course creation, a *'Ready-To-Go'* selling strategy is paramount for successful course marketing. Such a strategy empowers course creators to identify and reach their target audience effectively, crafting marketing content that resonates with potential students and increasing the likelihood of successful sales. By developing a clear selling strategy, course creators can create a consistent brand message and implement an impactful marketing campaign, bolstering the course's overall impact and visibility in the competitive online education market.

Moreover, a well-crafted selling strategy allows course creators to differentiate their courses from others, emphasizing unique selling points that attract more attention and engagement from potential students. Having a concrete plan of action and staying organized increases the chances of success, as course creators can take informed steps to promote and sell their courses, leading to more favorable outcomes.

A well-structured selling strategy enables course creators to replicate successful marketing campaigns, reaching new audiences and facilitating business growth over time. This scalability provides avenues for revenue expansion, contributing to the venture's long-term success.

Building a stronger brand image becomes achievable with a consistent brand message and voice facilitated by the selling strategy, contributing to greater brand recognition and reputation among the target audience.

Measuring success is a crucial aspect of any selling strategy, and with clear goals and metrics, course creators can track progress, make data-driven decisions, and continually improve their sales performance.

For those with a sales team, the selling strategy provides a clear roadmap for effective sales, ensuring everyone is aligned with the same goals and sales approach, enhancing overall efficiency and results.

Understanding customer needs and pain points is essential for creating courses that better meet their requirements, leading to higher customer satisfaction, positive reviews, and an enhanced reputation within the industry. A strong selling strategy can positively influence other aspects of the business, such as product development, customer service, and operations, contributing to an overall improvement in the business strategy.

Chapter 15: Solutions Built for You

The COVID-19 pandemic has instigated profound changes in curriculum implementation, driven not only by the shift to online platforms but also by the heightened relevance of specific knowledge and skills in the current context.

Addressing these changes poses challenges for educational systems, institutions, and educators at large. It entails decision-making and resource allocation to adjust and prioritize curricula, ensuring content remains pertinent during emergencies, and securing consensus among all stakeholders.

Furthermore, these adjustments must prioritize the competencies and values that have come to the forefront during this crisis, including solidarity, self-directed learning, care for oneself and others, social-emotional skills, health, and resilience. Deciding on criteria and approaches for learning priorities and adjustments can be complex and contentious.

Focusing on Relevant Curricular Content

One approach involves focusing on more relevant curricular content and prioritizing it over others. Another approach integrates content and learning objectives into interdisciplinary thematic clusters addressing multiple subjects simultaneously, fostering a comprehensive and connected learning experience.

Promoting this approach necessitates valuing teachers' independence and encouraging the development of complex competencies among educators.

Some countries have proposed curriculum prioritization plans with reduced fundamental learning objectives across different disciplines, moving towards a modular content approach by level, transitioning from basic education to new learning linked to integrated or significant objectives establishing connections between subjects.

Curriculum Adaptation

Curriculum adaptation, flexibility, and contextualization should prioritize learning objectives and content that enhance understanding and response to crises. This includes elements related to care and health, critical and reflective thinking regarding information and news, understanding social and economic trends, and promoting empathetic, tolerant, and non-discriminative behavior. Additionally, adjustments must cater to the needs of specific groups, such as students with disabilities or those facing challenging living conditions that hinder their ability to continue their studies.

Addressing linguistic and cultural diversity among diverse populations and indigenous communities is essential. Moreover, adopting a gender perspective is crucial to identify and eliminate situations of gender inequality or violence that may exacerbate during challenging circumstances.

Transitioning with the Times

As many countries have transitioned to online learning resources for educational continuity, the internet presents a unique opportunity to bridge the gap between schools and or educators and students, particularly in difficult circumstances.

However, unequal access to online learning opportunities can widen pre-existing gaps in access to information and knowledge, hinder socialization and inclusion, and impede the learning process that distance education aims to provide. Policymakers must recognize the multidimensional nature of social inequalities and work intentionally to reverse them, ensuring equal access to technology for disadvantaged populations.

Important Assessments

Furthermore, online learning activities highlight the importance of assessments in the formative role of learning. Diagnostic and follow-up exercises enable teachers to gather information about individual student learning, providing valuable feedback and adapting teaching strategies to enhance effectiveness.

Formative assessment and self-assessment instruments facilitate a collaborative evaluation process between teachers and students, promoting progress toward intended learning outcomes.

Benefits of Online Education Solutions

Amidst technological advancements, online education solutions have emerged as a promising way to create a conducive learning environment.

The following are some of the most notable benefits:

Flexibility and Autonomy

Unlike traditional classroom methods, online learning offers flexibility and autonomy, allowing students to take control of their learning schedule. This is particularly advantageous for working individuals who can't attend classes in person, as they can now access a wide range of online courses, degrees, and certifications at their convenience.

Interactive Models and Digital Simulations

These enhance comprehension of complex concepts, and technology has made learning more engaging and enjoyable through diverse learning tasks that improve retention of new knowledge. Frequent assessments interspersed with multimedia content contribute to improved student engagement and content retention.

Cost Saving Benefits

Moreover, online education solutions offer cost-saving benefits for educational institutions. By reducing classroom-based resources and manpower, educational institutes can scale their services and improve accessibility to education.

Embracing technology in the form of online education solutions opens up new opportunities for learners and allows institutions to adapt and grow continually.

The Benefits of Upskilling Educators

In the dynamic landscape of online education, educators play a pivotal role in shaping the learning experience for students. As technology continues to advance and teaching methodologies evolve, the need for upskilling educators becomes paramount. Online learning solutions provide a fertile ground for educators to acquire new skills and enhance their professional development in several key areas:

Curriculum Implementation

With the integration of technology into education, educators can explore innovative methods for curriculum design and implementation. They can learn to leverage digital tools, interactive resources, and learning management systems to create engaging and effective online courses. This upskilling empowers them to adapt to changing pedagogical approaches and cater to diverse learning styles.

Leadership Development

Online learning solutions extend beyond the classroom, offering educators opportunities for leadership development. They can engage in courses and programs that focus on educational leadership, administration, and management. These skills are valuable for those aspiring to take on leadership roles within educational institutions or contribute to the strategic direction of online learning initiatives.

Policymaking and Educational Technology

Understanding the intersection of education policy and technology is vital in the digital age. Educators can explore courses that delve into developing and implementing educational technology policies, data privacy regulations, and ethical considerations. This knowledge equips them to navigate the regulatory landscape and advocate for sound policies in the online learning sphere.

Lifelong Learning and Adaptation

The field of education is dynamic, with continuous advancements in pedagogy and technology. Upskilling educators in the art of lifelong learning and adaptation is crucial. They can develop strategies for staying updated with emerging trends, attending online workshops and conferences, and engaging with professional learning communities. This mindset of continual growth benefits both educators and their students.

Collaboration and Peer Learning

Online learning solutions foster a sense of global connectivity among educators. They can collaborate with peers from diverse backgrounds, sharing insights, best practices, and innovative approaches to teaching. Peer learning enriches their professional development journey and expands their perspectives on effective online instruction.

Educators can embark on their upskilling journey through a variety of avenues. Many educational institutions offer professional development programs tailored to online teaching. Additionally, online platforms and learning management systems provide access to many courses, webinars, and resources. Educators can choose self-paced learning or participate in structured programs, depending on their preferences and schedules.

In essence, upskilling educators in the digital age enhances their capabilities and enriches the online learning ecosystem. It ensures that students receive high-quality education delivered by well-equipped educators to harness the potential of online learning solutions. As technology continues to shape the future of education, the commitment to professional growth remains a cornerstone of effective online instruction.

Personalized Learning

Online learning solutions enable educators to experience personalized learning first-hand. They can explore adaptive learning platforms and adaptive assessment tools, gaining insights into how personalized learning benefits students. This knowledge empowers them to tailor their instruction to individual student needs effectively.

Blended Learning Strategies

Educators can delve into the realm of blended learning, combining both online and in-person teaching methods. They can learn to create seamless transitions between physical and digital classrooms, maximizing the benefits of both modalities for enhanced student engagement and outcomes.

Data Analysis and Assessment

Proficiency in data analysis is a valuable skill for educators. They can upskill in interpreting student data, identifying trends, and using analytics to inform instructional decisions. This data-driven approach enables educators to provide targeted support and optimize learning experiences.

Inclusive Education

Educators can explore inclusive education practices in the online environment. They can learn strategies to accommodate diverse learners, including those with disabilities. This upskilling fosters an inclusive and equitable online learning ecosystem.

Tech Integration

Online learning solutions often involve the integration of various educational technologies. Educators can upskill in selecting, implementing, and effectively using digital tools in their teaching. This proficiency enhances the learning experience for students and streamlines administrative tasks.

Research and Pedagogy

Educators can use research-based pedagogical courses to align their teaching strategies with the latest educational research findings. Staying informed about evidence-based practices ensures that educators deliver effective online instruction.

Ethical Considerations

Online educators should be well-versed in ethical considerations related to technology use and online teaching. They can explore topics such as digital citizenship, online safety, and responsible use of educational technology.

Mentoring and Coaching

Experienced educators can upskill in mentoring and coaching techniques to support their colleagues who may be new to online teaching. This collaborative approach strengthens the overall teaching community.

Educational Trends and Innovation

Keeping abreast of educational trends and innovative practices is essential. Educators can engage with thought leaders, attend online conferences, and explore emerging educational technologies to remain at the forefront of their field.

Incorporating these aspects into their professional development journey empowers educators to thrive in the digital age. It positions them as catalysts for positive change in education, enabling students to access high-quality, innovative, and responsive online learning experiences.

Ultimately, upskilling educators is an investment in their individual growth and a commitment to enhancing the quality of education for all learners. As technology continues to reshape education, educators who embrace the opportunities for upskilling are better equipped to navigate the digital frontier and lead the way toward a brighter future for online learning.

The Challenge of Access

One of the primary challenges students may encounter in the realm of online learning is access to specific applications required for virtual learning sessions. Limited facilities or unreliable internet connectivity may hinder their ability to download information, resulting in blurry videos and restricted communication with teachers.

Time Management and Persistence

Time management can be another hurdle as some concepts may demand more time to grasp fully, and intermittent internet issues can disrupt the learning process. Balancing flexible schedules with recurring learning sessions can be challenging, making it imperative for learners to prioritize tasks and minimize distractions to meet learning outcomes.

Motivation is the cornerstone for consistent engagement in online learning. Students must maintain consistent effort in attending all learning activities and completing assignments to achieve success.

Effective Communication and Collaboration

Effective communication is critical in the online learning environment. Students should actively interact with their peers and educators to improve their communication skills and overcome potential barriers to learning.

Collaborative activities, group discussions, and interactive assignments can enhance the sense of community among online learners.

Adapting to the Digital Era

As we continue to navigate the digital era, it's crucial to recognize that online education solutions have evolved to address many of the challenges they initially presented.

Educational institutions and or educators are increasingly investing in technology infrastructure, ensuring that students from various backgrounds have equitable access to online resources.

Innovation in Pedagogy

The majority of educators are continually innovating in pedagogy to make online learning more engaging and effective. They leverage multimedia content, interactive simulations, and gamified learning experiences to enhance student comprehension and retention. Frequent assessments interspersed with these engaging elements contribute to improved student engagement and content retention.

Cost-Efficiency for Educational Institutions

Moreover, online education solutions offer cost-saving benefits for educational institutions and educators themselves. By reducing the need for physical classroom resources and manpower, educational institutes can scale their services and improve access to education. Embracing technology in the form of online education solutions opens up new opportunities for learners and allows institutions to adapt and grow continually.

Overcoming Challenges through Collaboration

The success of online education also relies on collaboration. Educational institutions, governments, and technology providers must work together to bridge the digital divide.

Policies that promote equal access to technology and internet infrastructure are essential to ensure that no student is left behind in the digital age.

Personal Responsibility in Online Learning

While institutions and educators play a vital role in delivering quality online education, students also bear responsibility. Online learners must proactively manage their time, stay motivated, and actively participate in their courses. Effective time management, communication, and self-discipline are key skills for success in online learning.

A Dynamic Educational Landscape

The world of education is evolving rapidly, and online learning is at the forefront of this transformation. As technology continues to advance, online education will become even more accessible, interactive, and effective. It will adapt to the needs of diverse learners, offering flexibility and personalization to meet individual educational goals.

Meeting the Diverse Needs of Learners

Online education's flexibility also extends to learners with diverse needs. It can accommodate students with disabilities, those facing challenging living conditions, or individuals who require a more personalized learning approach. Addressing linguistic and cultural diversity among diverse populations and indigenous communities is crucial to ensure inclusive access to quality education.

Additionally, adopting a gender perspective is essential to identify and eliminate situations of gender inequality or violence that may be exacerbated during challenging circumstances.

Uneven Impact and Educational Inequalities

The pandemic has unevenly impacted the implementation of curricula across different education levels. Learning achievement differences are expected to be exacerbated due to existing educational inequalities and uneven access to curriculum coverage. Policymakers and educators must pay particular attention to addressing these disparities and providing support to students who may have been disproportionately affected.

Leveraging Technology for Inclusivity

Despite these challenges, the Internet presents a unique opportunity to bridge the gap between schools and students, particularly in difficult circumstances. It can serve as a powerful equalizer, provided policymakers recognize social inequalities' multidimensional nature and work intentionally to reverse them. Ensuring equal access to technology for disadvantaged populations is essential to achieving educational inclusivity.

Challenges in Online Learning

However, online learning is not without its challenges. Students may face obstacles such as the need for specific applications for virtual learning sessions, limited facilities, or internet connectivity issues that can result in blurred videos and restricted communication with teachers. Time management can also be difficult, as some concepts may require more time to understand, and intermittent internet problems can disrupt the learning process. Balancing flexible schedules with repetitive learning sessions can be challenging, making it important for learners to prioritize and avoid distractions to meet learning outcomes.

Motivation is essential for consistent engagement in online learning, and students must consistently attend all learning activities and assignments. Effective communication is crucial, and students should actively interact with peers and educators to improve their communication skills and overcome barriers to learning.

The Future of Online Learning

In short, online learning has become a vital component of the education landscape, offering a dynamic and flexible approach to learning. It has proven its value during times of crisis and will continue to play a significant role in education.

As technology advances and educational institutions adapt, online learning will become even more accessible, interactive, and effective. It will cater to the diverse needs of learners, bridge educational inequalities, and empower students and educators alike.

Online learning holds the promise of a brighter future for education, where knowledge knows no bounds and access is truly universal.

Closing Thoughts on Online Education

In the ever-evolving landscape of education, online learning stands as a transformative force, offering boundless possibilities for students, educators, and institutions. Its adaptability and resilience have been demonstrated during times of crisis, ensuring that learning can continue even in the face of adversity.

As we look to the future, it is clear that online education will remain an integral part of the educational ecosystem. The flexibility it provides, the opportunities for personalization and engagement, and the potential for bridging educational inequalities make it a powerful tool for advancing education on a global scale.

However, as online learning continues to evolve, it is essential to address its challenges, such as ensuring equitable access, overcoming technical obstacles, and maintaining motivation and engagement. These challenges can be surmounted with thoughtful planning, innovative solutions, and a commitment to inclusivity.

In the end, online education holds the promise of a more accessible, flexible, and personalized learning experience for all. It empowers individuals to pursue knowledge regardless of geographical constraints or personal circumstances. It fosters a lifelong love of learning and equips students with the skills and knowledge they need to thrive in a rapidly changing world.

As we embark on this educational journey, let us embrace the opportunities that online learning affords and work together to build a future where education truly knows no boundaries. The future of learning is here, and it is bright with possibilities.

Summary

The COVID-19 pandemic has accelerated the shift to online education. This poses challenges for educational systems to adjust and prioritize curricula while securing consensus among stakeholders. Adjustments should focus on competencies like resilience, social-emotional skills, and promoting tolerance.

Approaches include prioritizing relevant curricular content, integrating objectives across subjects, and curriculum adaptation to enhance crisis understanding. Technology provides opportunities to bridge gaps, but unequal access can exacerbate inequalities.

Online learning benefits include flexibility, engaging digital tools, and cost savings for institutions. However, challenges remain around access, time management, motivation, and communication. Collaboration between institutions, governments, and providers is key to overcoming barriers.

Looking ahead, online learning will continue advancing and adapting to learner needs. It can promote inclusivity if policymakers address unequal access. While not without challenges, online education provides a dynamic, flexible learning experience that empowers students and educators alike. Overall, it holds promise for making education more accessible worldwide.

Ready to Grab Toolkit
A Simplified Framework on How to Create, Sell, and Teach Online Courses! Winning Techniques to Help You Create, Sell, and Impart Your Knowledge and Expertise Online

Navigating the Online Education Landscape

The digital age has reshaped education and learning. The internet and technology have connected us globally and transformed how we acquire knowledge and skills. Online courses, in particular, have become a powerful means of sharing knowledge, skills, and expertise in a dynamic and accessible manner.

Whether you're an educator looking to expand your reach, an expert eager to share your specialized knowledge, or an entrepreneur seeking new revenue streams, this comprehensive toolkit, presented within this book, offers simplified yet invaluable guidance. It paves a clear and structured path to help you create, sell, and teach online courses while navigating the ever-evolving digital learning landscape.

Online education holds boundless potential, enabling you to transcend geographical boundaries and connect with a global audience. However, to make a significant impact, you need more than just content; you need a strategic approach. This framework empowers you with a range of winning techniques to successfully harness online education's vast potential.

With this toolkit, you'll embark on a journey that combines your expertise, passion, and dedication with the latest technology and educational methodologies. Together, we'll explore the multifaceted world of online courses, from identifying your niche and crafting compelling content to marketing your courses effectively and providing ongoing learner support. You'll learn how to scale your online course business, adapt to industry changes, and ensure legal and ethical compliance.

Embarking on the Online Education Journey: A Comprehensive Guide

Prepare for a transformative voyage into the realm of online education. The path may be challenging, but the rewards in knowledge dissemination, financial growth, and personal fulfillment are immeasurable. With the right strategies, tools, and determination, you can unlock the doors to a world where learning knows no bounds, and your expertise can reach and inspire individuals around the globe. So, let's dive in and explore the exciting universe of online course creation and delivery together, utilizing the following sections:

Section 1: Identifying Your Niche and Expertise

- Define Your Expertise: Assess your skills, knowledge, and passion to identify your niche.

- Target Audience: Understand your potential students or customers and their needs.

- Market Research: Analyze the demand for your expertise in the online learning market.

Section 2: Course Creation and Content Development

- Learning Objectives: Define clear, measurable learning outcomes for your course.

- Curriculum Design: Structure your course content logically and sequentially.

- Content Creation: Develop engaging and valuable course materials, including videos, written content, quizzes, and assignments.

- Multimedia Production: Tips for creating high-quality videos and graphics.

- Interactive Learning: Incorporate discussion forums, live Q&A sessions, and group projects for a dynamic learning experience.

- Assessment and Evaluation: Design effective quizzes and assignments to measure student progress.

Section 3: Building Your Online Course Platform

- Choose a Learning Management System (LMS): Compare popular LMS options and select the one that suits your needs.

- Website Setup: Create a professional and user-friendly course website.

- E-commerce Integration: Set up secure payment gateways for selling courses.

- User Experience: Optimize the online learning platform for easy navigation and accessibility.

Section 4: Pricing Strategies and Marketing

- Pricing Models: Decide between one-time payments, subscriptions, or freemium models.

- Marketing Plan: Develop a comprehensive strategy to reach your target audience.

- SEO and Content Marketing: Optimize your content for search engines and leverage content marketing to attract organic traffic.

- Email Marketing: Use an email list to promote your courses.

- Social Media Promotion: Use various social media platforms to engage with your audience.

- Affiliate Marketing: Collaborate with affiliates to extend your course's reach.

Section 5: Teaching and Engaging Your Students

- Effective Teaching Techniques: Learn how to engage, motivate, and educate your students effectively.

- Student Support: Assist in discussion forums, emails, or live sessions.

- Continuous Improvement: Gather feedback and data to enhance your courses over time.

Section 6: Scaling Your Online Course

- Automation: Implement automation tools to handle administrative tasks efficiently, allowing you to focus on core aspects of your business.

- Expanding Course Catalog: Diversify your course offerings by creating additional courses, catering to a broader audience, and increasing revenue streams.

- Scaling Marketing Efforts: Reach a wider audience by diversifying your marketing channels, ensuring your courses are accessible to a global audience.

- Collaboration and Partnerships: Explore collaboration opportunities with influencers, fellow educators, or other industry experts. Such collaborations can extend your course's reach and credibility while providing unique perspectives and insights.

- Outsourcing: Consider outsourcing certain tasks such as customer support, marketing, or technical support to efficiently manage the increasing demands of your expanding business, allowing you to focus on strategic growth.

Section 7: Monitoring and Analytics

- Track Student Progress: Use analytics to monitor student engagement and progress in your courses.

- Identify Drop-Off Points: Analyze where students commonly disengage or drop out and make improvements accordingly.

- Data-Driven Decision Making: Use data to refine your course content, marketing strategies, and teaching methods.

Section 8: Handling Technical Challenges

- Technical Support: Offer assistance to students who encounter technical issues during the course.

- Troubleshooting: Prepare guides and FAQs to help students resolve common technical problems.

- Regular Updates: Keep your course platform and content up to date to prevent technical issues.

Section 9: Feedback Loops

- Gather Student Feedback: Regularly solicit feedback from your students to improve your courses.

- Iterative Course Development: Use feedback to make incremental changes and enhancements to your course content.

- Feedback on Marketing: Understand the most effective marketing strategies through student feedback.

Section 10: Legal, Compliance, and Intellectual Property Considerations

- Copyright and Intellectual Property: Develop a comprehensive understanding of the legal considerations involved in creating and selling online courses covering copyright and intellectual property issues.

- Privacy and Data Protection: Guarantee that your courses adhere to privacy and data protection regulations, ensuring the protection of both your students and your business.

- Using Intellectual Property: Comprehend the legal considerations when incorporating copyrighted material, trademarks, and intellectual property within your courses.

- Data Protection Compliance: Ensure full compliance with data protection regulations, particularly when collecting and managing student data.

- Terms and Conditions: Create transparent and comprehensive terms and conditions for both your courses and website, establishing a clear and equitable framework for your students.

- Copyright and Fair Use: Ensure that you avoid copyright infringement when using third-party materials in your courses.

- Ethical Marketing: Practice ethical marketing principles and steer clear of deceptive tactics.

Section 11: Marketing and Promotion

- Content Marketing: Leverage blog posts, articles, and videos to promote your courses and establish yourself as an expert in your field.

- Email Marketing: To effectively target potential students, build and segment your email list.

- Social Media Marketing: Utilize various social media platforms to engage with your audience and promote your courses.

- Paid Advertising: Consider pay-per-click (PPC) advertising on platforms like Google Ads and social media to reach a wider audience.

- Affiliate Marketing: Partner with affiliates who promote your courses in exchange for a commission on sales.

- Webinars and Seminars: Host free webinars and seminars to showcase your expertise and attract potential students.

Section 12: Course Updates and Maintenance

- Regular Content Updates: Keep your courses fresh by updating them with new information and insights.

- Maintain Technical Functionality: Ensure your courses work smoothly on all devices and platforms.

- Customer Support: Continue to provide excellent customer support as your courses evolve.

Section 13: Measuring Success

- Key Performance Indicators (KPIs): Define and track KPIs to measure the success of your online course business.

- Financial Metrics: Monitor revenue, expenses, and profitability to make informed business decisions.

- Student Feedback: Gather feedback from students to assess their satisfaction and make improvements.

Section 14: Evolving with the Industry

- Stay Informed: Keep an eye on industry trends, emerging technologies, and changes in student preferences.

- Adapt and Innovate: Be prepared to adapt your courses and teaching methods to remain competitive in the online education landscape.

- Professional Development: Invest in your own education and skills to stay at the forefront of your subject area and teaching techniques.

Section 15: Case Studies and Success Stories

- Share examples of successful online course creators who have achieved substantial growth and recognition in the field.

Section 16: Community Building and Engagement

- Student Forums: Explore the idea of creating discussion forums or online communities where students can interact, collaborate, and support one another.

- Feedback Loops: Encourage students to actively provide feedback and suggestions, creating a continuous feedback loop to enhance the quality of your courses.

- Networking Events: Host virtual events that bring students and course creators together for networking, collaboration, and exchanging ideas.

- The Role of Community: Gain insights into the role of a strong online community, understanding how it can benefit both you and your students.

- Tools and Platforms: Learn about the various platforms and tools available for building and effectively managing online communities, ensuring a seamless and engaging experience for your students.

Section 17: Online Course Marketplaces

- Explore opportunities to sell your courses on established online course marketplaces, such as edX, Udemy, Coursera, or eLearningX.

- Understand the pros and cons of using these platforms, including revenue-sharing and limitations on course customization.

Section 18: Special Considerations

- International Audiences: Tailor your courses to appeal to a global audience, including language considerations.

- Accessibility: Ensure your courses are accessible to individuals with disabilities, complying with accessibility standards.

- Course Pricing Strategies: Evaluate different pricing models, including one-time payments, subscriptions, or tiered access levels.

- Strategies for Nonprofits and Educational Institutions: Learn how to adapt your approach if you are targeting nonprofit organizations or traditional educational institutions.

- Continuing Education and Certifications: Explore opportunities to offer certificates or continuing education credits in your courses.

- Handling Technical Challenges: Prepare for potential technical issues like platform downtime or server crashes.

Section 19: Self-Care and Well-Being

- Maintaining Work-Life Balance: Find a balance between managing your online course business and personal well-being.

- Handling Stress and Burnout: Develop strategies to cope with the demands and pressure of course creation and management.

- Support Systems: Build a support network of mentors, peers, or coaches who can provide guidance and encouragement.

Section 20: Success Stories and Interviews

- Share interviews with successful online course creators and educators who can provide insights, tips, and inspiration.

- SEO and Content Strategy: Optimize your website and course content for search engines to increase your online visibility.

Section 21: Student Acquisition and Retention

- Strategies for Attracting Students: Learn techniques for reaching a wider audience and converting them into paying students.

- Student Onboarding: Create a seamless onboarding process to help students get started with their courses.

- Student Retention: Discover methods for keeping students engaged and motivated throughout their learning journey.

Section 22: Analytics and Data Analysis

- Using Analytics Tools: Understand how to utilize analytics tools to gather insights into student behavior and course performance.

- Data-Driven Decision Making: Make informed decisions based on the data you collect, such as adjusting course content or marketing strategies.

Section 23: Scaling Your Business

- Automating Processes: Implement automation tools to handle repetitive tasks and scale your operations.

- Hiring and Team Building: Explore options for expanding your team to manage growth efficiently.

- Expanding Your Course Catalog: Tips for creating additional courses and diversifying your offerings.

Section 24: Monetization Strategies

- Beyond Course Sales: Explore alternative revenue streams, such as affiliate marketing, consulting, or speaking engagements.

- Subscription Models: Consider offering membership or subscription-based access to your courses.

Section 25: Public Speaking and Webinars

- Leveraging Webinars: Discover how webinars can be used for promoting your courses and engaging with your audience.

- Presentation Skills: Learn techniques for effective public speaking and engaging your audience.

Section 26: Course Feedback and Iteration

- Gathering Student Feedback: Explore strategies for collecting and analyzing feedback from students.

- Iteration and Improvement: Continually refine your courses based on feedback and changing educational trends.

Section 27: Networking and Collaborations

- Partnering with Influencers: Collaborate with influencers or experts in your field to expand your reach.

- Affiliate Marketing: Understand how affiliate marketing can drive course sales through partnerships.

Section 28: International Expansion

- Localizing Content: Strategies for adapting your courses for international markets.

- Payment Processing and Legal Considerations: Navigate international payment methods and legal requirements.

Section 29: The Future of Online Education

- Emerging Trends: Explore current and future trends in online education, including new technologies, learning formats, and markets.

- Preparing for the Future: Strategies for staying at the forefront of the eLearning industry.

Section 30: Case Studies and Real-Life Examples

- Share real-life case studies of successful online course creators, highlighting their journeys, challenges, and achievements.

Section 31: Compliance and Regulations

- Data Protection: Understand data privacy laws and ensure your course platform complies with them.

- Accessibility: Ensure your courses are accessible to individuals with disabilities, complying with accessibility standards.

Section 32: Creating Effective Assessments

- Types of Assessments: Explore different assessment methods, including quizzes, assignments, and peer reviews.

- Grading and Feedback: Tips for providing constructive feedback and grading assignments efficiently.

Section 33: Dealing with Technical Issues

- Troubleshooting: Prepare for common technical challenges students might face and provide solutions.

- Support Systems: Develop a robust support system to promptly assist students with technical issues.

Section 34: Personal Branding

- Building Your Personal Brand: Strategies for establishing yourself as an expert in your niche.

- Online Presence: Enhance your online presence through social media, blogging, and other platforms.

Section 35: Measuring Success

- Key Performance Indicators (KPIs): Identify the metrics to track your course's performance.

- Setting Goals: Establish clear, measurable goals for your courses and your business.

Section 36: Responding to Market Changes

- Adapting to Market Trends: Keep your courses aligned with the market's ever-changing demands.

- Competitive Analysis: Continuously analyze the competition to maintain a competitive edge.

Section 37: Handling Customer Support

- Providing Effective Support: Tips for offering responsive customer support for student queries and concerns.

- Crisis Management: Prepare for handling difficult situations or student complaints.

Section 38: Public Relations and Marketing

- Influencer Partnerships: Collaborate with influencers to reach wider audiences.

- Crisis Communication: Manage public relations during critical situations.

Section 39: Balancing Entrepreneurship and Education

- Maintaining Quality: Ensure the quality of your educational content while growing your business.

- Work-Life Balance: Strategies for balancing the demands of entrepreneurship and personal life.

Section 40: Adapting to Learning Trends

- Microlearning and Mobile Learning: Incorporate microlearning and mobile-friendly course elements.

- Gamification and Interactivity: Use gamified elements and interactivity to enhance the learning experience.

Section 41: Honing Presentation Skills

- Effective Communication: Improve your ability to communicate complex topics clearly.

- Storytelling Techniques: Use storytelling to engage and motivate your students.

Section 42: Crowdsourcing and Collaborative Course Creation

- Engaging Students in Content Creation: Explore collaborative learning approaches where students contribute to course content.

- Crowdsourced Feedback: Gather feedback from your audience to improve your courses.

Section 43: Post-Course Engagement and Upselling

- Continuing Education: Encourage students to continue their learning journey through advanced courses or memberships.

- Post-Course Support: Offer ongoing support and resources to keep students engaged.

Section 44: Ethical Considerations in Online Education

- Plagiarism and Academic Honesty: Promote ethical behavior and enforce policies to prevent plagiarism.

- Online Safety: Ensure a safe and respectful learning environment by addressing inappropriate behavior.

Section 45: Exit Strategies

- Preparing for Exit: Understand how to plan for the eventual sale of your online course business or transition into retirement.

Summary

This comprehensive toolkit guides creating, selling, and teaching online courses in the digital age. It caters to educators, experts, and entrepreneurs, offering 45 online course creation and management sections.

Starting with identifying your expertise, understanding your audience, and conducting market research, the toolkit guides you in creating engaging course content and setting up your online course platform. It also delves into pricing and marketing strategies.

The toolkit explores teaching techniques, student engagement, and scaling your course business while addressing aspects like monitoring and analytics, technical challenges, feedback loops, legal compliance, and ethical marketing. It offers insights into marketing and promotion, course maintenance, and measuring success.

Adaptation to industry changes, case studies, and community engagement are emphasized. You'll learn how to leverage online course marketplaces, deal with special considerations, and prioritize your well-being. Monetization, public speaking, and effective feedback mechanisms are also covered.

Networking, international expansion, and future trends in online education are discussed. The toolkit presents success stories, compliance with regulations, efficient assessment methods, addressing technical issues, personal branding, and measuring success. It additionally guides you on responding to market changes, offering customer support, handling public relations, balancing entrepreneurship with education, and staying current with learning trends.

Finally, it touches on crowdsourcing, post-course engagement, ethical considerations, and exit strategies for your online course business. In sum, this toolkit equips you with the knowledge and strategies needed to excel in the realm of online education.